CONTENTS

CHAMPIONS

MAY 11 1991: RANGERS 2 ABERDEEN 0

It was a day that, in years and decades to come, Rangers fans will proudly relate to their grandchildren: "I was there!".

It was a day when the atmosphere inside Ibrox Stadium was quite unbelievable, quite fantastic, quite superb — a day when the Rangers fans played a magnificent part in the outcome of the game, as they roared their heroes on to the ultimate triumph.

And yet . . . the odds had seemed so much against Rangers on the morning of May 11th. Eight points had been lost in the preceding ten league games, including a 0-1 reversal at Pittodrie on March 2nd, and a seemingly catastrophic 0-3 defeat at Motherwell, a result which to all intents and purposes left Aberdeen in the driving seat, requiring only one point at Ibrox to clinch the title.

Rangers could scarcely have been more ill-prepared for this crucial hour. Richard Gough, Trevor Steven and Oleg Kuznetsov were all absent through illness and injury, and many others, including substitutes Ally McCoist and Ian Durrant, were less than 100% fit.

Indeed, there can be no doubt that the critical injury crisis at Ibrox had been a major factor in the Championship run-in. No fewer than eight first-team players had been long-term absentees during the season — a daunting handicap for any club, no matter how strong the squad.

Aberdeen came to Ibrox very much in form, having dropped only one League point since January 19th and with a settled team, packed solid with experienced men who had been over the course before — Alex McLeish, Stewart

McKimmie, Jim Bett, Robert Connor and Hans Gillhaus. Was it conceivable that a side of such quality could freeze on such a big occasion?

The tension was so thick on that memorable afternoon you could have cut it with a knife. The atmosphere so electric — and yet many Rangers fans in the stadium questioned the team selection. Manager Walter Smith had clearly gone for experience.

Time would prove him right . . .

Rangers seized the initiative from the kick-off, with Mark Hateley challenging young Dons keeper Michael Watt (replacing the injured Theo Snelders) for a high ball, only for Mark Walters to pass-up a golden opportunity from the loose ball.

Left: Mark Hateley opens the scoring with a superb aerial strike: and the squad celebrate with the Championship trophy. Right: What a smacker! Maurice Johnston congratulates Hateley on his golden goal.

CHAMPIONS

Aberdeen seemed to wilt under the phenomenal wall of sound, but gradually regained their composure and scorned a glorious opportunity to take the lead in 19 minutes, when Pieter Van de Ven, clean through, shot tamely straight at Chris Woods.

Rangers suffered a blow four minutes later, when Tom Cowan was stretchered off with a broken leg to be replaced by Ian Durrant, and Hans Gillhaus became the second Dutchman to miss a clear chance, heading over from close-in.

Aberdeen, nevertheless, seemed in command, until the turning-point of perhaps the entire season arrived in 40 minutes — a moment that will live forever in the minds eye of those present.

Mark Walters seemed boxed in on the left touchline, but somehow swung in a high cross for Mark Hateley to leap high above Alex McLeish and power home an explosive header that left the goalkeeper helpless.

The stadium erupted in a joyous sea of blue and you sensed that the tide had turned . . .

It was Hateley again in 58 minutes who pounced when Watt failed to hold a Maurice Johnston shot, and Rangers were 2-0 ahead as the light blue legions, to put it mildly, went berserk . . .!

The injury jinx struck once more to haunt the Ibrox men, when John Brown was carried off, to be substituted by a scarcely-fit Ally McCoist, with 20 minutes left.

Rangers now had a back four of Nisbet, Stevens, Spackman and Hurlock, not one of whom was playing in their natural position. Time seemed to stand still as Aberdeen poured forward in droves. Rangers were left with barely six fit men, as all the injuries took their toll. Many fans could scarcely watch, although in reality Chris Woods was seldom tested and the final whistle sounded to mark Rangers' 41st League Championship, on a day when all thirteen players truly "played for the jersey".

Every man had been a hero, but perhaps special mention should go to Mark Hateley for his two goals; to Gary Stevens, who played superbly well in three different positions; to Nigel Spackman, an inspiring captain on the day; and to Maurice Johnston, whose sterling performance covered every inch of the pitch.

Above all else, special mention to the 37,652 spectators, who created an atmosphere that will long be remembered and to the Ibrox Legions who carried their team to one of the greatest victories in Rangers' long and proud history.

TEAMS

RANGERS: Woods, Stevens, Cowan (Durrant), Nisbet, Spackman, Brown (McCoist), Hurlock, Ferguson, Hateley, Johnston, Walters.

ABERDEEN: Watt, Wright, Robertson, Grant, McLeish, McKimmie, Van de Ven (Van der Ark) Bett, Jess (Booth), Connor, Gillhaus.

Above: It's man of the match Hateley again as he coolly slots in number two to tie the game up. Below: Bubbly in the bath for Maurice Johnston and Ian Durrant — and well deserved too!

Player Profile

IAN DURRANT

ON April 6th 1991, Ian Durrant stepped out of a long, dark tunnel into the light that was Ibrox Stadium.

Two-and-a-half years of shadow had ended at last — 30 months of pain and suffering, of hard work and dedication, were at last consigned to memory.

The victim of a crippling tackle by Aberdeen's Neil Simpson at Pittodrie on October 8th 1988, which seemed at the time to have compromised his career entirely, Durrant's was a supreme talent seemingly cut down in its prime.

A local boy from Govan, Ian joined Rangers as a schoolboy from Glasgow United and progressed

Left: Ian in his comeback game against Hibs, showing all his old skill to Gordon Hunter. Below: A great moment as Ian scores against St Johnstone.

rapidly through the ranks winning Scottish international honours at youth, under-18, under-21 and full international level (on five occasions).

Primarily a midfielder, Durrant is a player of the highest quality — quick, skilful and well-balanced, with the ability and confidence to run at defences and the positional sense to "ghost-in" at the most opportune moment.

It was Jock Wallace who first introduced him to the Rangers top team, making his league debut in a 3-0 win at Greenock in season 1984/85, when a certain Alistair McCoist scored a hat-trick!

A regular from then on in the first-team, Durrant undoubtedly profited greatly from the arrival one year later of Graeme Souness as player-manager and over the next two years

Rangers fans glowed in sheer ecstasy as Durrant and Souness himself linked up in midfield with such class players as Ray Wilkins and Derek Ferguson.

A League Championship winner's medal in 1986/87 accompanied two League Cup "gongs" in '86/87 and '87/88, and what seemed set to be a glittering international career got under way in a 2-0 Hampden victory over Hungary in a friendly on September 9th 1987, with that man McCoist again on target with both goals!

Durrant could also score goals himself — most notably against Celtic — witness the superb one-two with Davie Cooper at Ibrox to score the only goal of the August 1986 league encounter, not to mention the opening goal in the League Cup Final some two months later.

And who could ever forget his decisive strike in the vital penalty shoot-out of the 1987/88 League Cup Final against Aberdeen?

A glorious career beckoned until that dreadful day at Aberdeen, when Durrant's right knee was shattered, the cruciate ligament severed and Scottish football held its collective breath.

An aborted comeback in February 1990 saw Durrant play three reserve fixtures before further complications set in, necessitating revolutionary surgery in the USA (in all, Ian had to undergo three major operations).

Finally, in January 1991, Durrant once again returned to the reserves, attracting a quite staggering 10,500 to his comeback match. This time there were to be no further hiccups and the first-team door beckoned for him at last on April 6th, with the Hibernian captain Andy Goram taking time out to offer his best wishes.

One week later, Durrant was on the score sheet in a 3-0 win over St Johnstone and although sitting out two games in the run-in, he played for 67 minutes in the league decider against Aberdeen — and how sweet that result must have seemed to him!

Welcome back, Ian. True football followers everywhere salute your bravery and courage — may your career yet be a long and successful one!

Ian Durrant shows the famous 'Cruyff turn' to Gareth Evans of Hibs in his comeback match.

Season	League	League Cup	Scottish Cup	Europe	Others	Total
1984/85	5	—	—	—	2(1)	7(1)
1985/86	30(2)	5	1(1)	1	8(2)	45(5)
1986/87	39(4)	5(1)	1	5(1)	8	58(6)
1987/88	40(10)	5(3)	3(2)	6(1)	9(1)	63(17)
1988/89	8(2)	4(1)	—	2(1)	4	18(4)
1990/91	4(1)	—	—	—	—	4(1)
Total	126(19)	19(5)	5(3)	14(3)	31(4)	195(34)

Figures in brackets represent goals scored.

CHANGES AT THE TOP

The news broke on the morning of Tuesday, April 16th 1991, rocking British football to its very foundations.

Graeme Souness was to resign as manager of Rangers Football Club in order to succeed his close friend, Kenny Dalglish, who resigned at Liverpool some two months earlier, for mainly personal reasons.

Rangers supporters everywhere were stunned.

It had, after all, only been six weeks since Graeme Souness had proclaimed his undying loyalty in the club newspaper, the 'Rangers News'.

Having at first declined the Liverpool offer, he accepted a second approach, but intended to delay his move until the end of the season.

Given that the story had now broken, this was clearly unacceptable, not least to David Murray, Chairman of Rangers, who, perhaps more than anyone else, had every right to feel betrayed. Nevertheless, it was he who came out of the entire affair with dignity and distinction, emphasising that here was a man to rank with the finest Rangers Chairmen.

"I think he's made the biggest mistake of his life," was Murray's most telling comment — and with those words a chapter in Rangers history closed.

How then, does one assess the Souness era?

His contribution to Rangers Football Club over the past five years should never be minimised. He pulled the club up from the abyss, turned it around quicker than anyone could have conceivably thought possible, attracted international stars to Ibrox Stadium that one could simply never have envisaged, and lifted

The fruits of success as Walter Smith and Archie Knox proudly hold the Championship trophy.

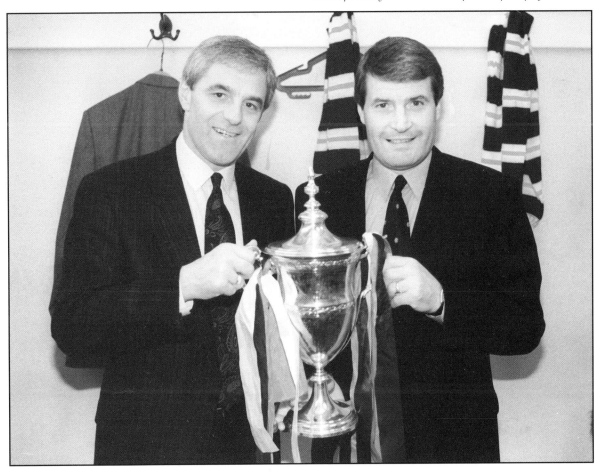

CHANGES AT THE TOP

Rangers onto a higher plane than at almost any other time in their history.

Admittedly, he had the financial backing to do so, but it must at least be questionable whether Rangers without Graeme Souness could have attracted the sponsorship and executive funding so crucial in this day and age.

And yet . . . the critics remain.

There were good times, there were bad times under Graeme Souness — but at the end of the day Rangers fans felt betrayed, unable to imagine a manager wanting to leave Ibrox for another club.

Somehow, one could never envisage Wilton, Struth, Symon, or Greig doing likewise. In conclusion, perhaps time will prove that the greatest contribution made by Graeme Souness to Rangers, was to introduce David Murray to the Club.

The immediate problem for Mr Murray and his directors upon Souness's departure was the question of a replacement — many names were the subject of press speculation, most notably Kenny Dalglish, George Graham, Alex Smith, and such rank outsiders as Ron Atkinson and Jack Charlton.

In reality, however, there was never any choice to be made as far as David Murray was concerned — assistant manager Walter Smith was appointed just three days later.

Most certainly, it was the kind of appointment that had served Liverpool so well during their glory years — Bill Shankly was succeeded by Bob Paisley, followed by Joe Fagan, and in turn by Kenny Dalglish.

Continuity was the basis of promotion from within, and it certainly hadn't served Rangers so badly when in 1920 manager William Wilton tragically drowned, and the club trainer took over the reins — a fellow by the name of William Struth.

Walter Smith's credentials were impeccable — widely respected as a coach, he had worked under Jim McLean, Jock Stein and Alex Ferguson, as well as Graeme Souness.

He first signed for Dundee United as an 18-year-old in November 1966 from Glasgow junior side Ashfield, playing at Tannadice for nine years before being transferred to Dumbarton in September 1975 for a £10,000 fee, then returning to United in January 1977 for £4,000.

Jim McLean encouraged his interest in the coaching side of football, and this was rewarded in March 1982 when he was appointed assistant manager at Tannadice, a post he would hold until the move to Ibrox in April 1986, just two months after being appointed a director of Dundee United F.C.

Recognition had come quickly at international level too. Named Scotland under-21 boss by Jock Stein in September 1984 after working as assistant to Andy Roxburgh with the under-18's for two years, he was finally appointed No 2 to Alex Ferguson in the build-up to the 1986 World Cup.

As a player, Walter Smith won very little in the way of honours, but he had been assistant to Jim McLean when Dundee United won the League Championship in season 1982/83, and he had shared in the success of the Souness years.

Indeed, perhaps the most telling comment of all came from captain Richard Gough when he commented on the Smith appointment, stating that it would make very little difference to the players as Walter had been doing almost all of the work anyway . . . !

To the Rangers fans, moreover, Walter Smith was a welcome appointment — he had been a Rangers fan all his life, and although never a player at Ibrox, was a manager in the Rangers tradition.

Smith's appointment was almost universally welcomed in footballing circles, his calm outward approach being more akin to what many people regard as being the true style of a Rangers manager.

Walter had served a long apprenticeship as No 2 at both Tannadice and Ibrox. His time had come, and most people recognised that here was a worthy successor to the distinguished line of Rangers managers.

Walter Smith's first appointment on taking over the reigns of office had to be his No 2. Any manager will stress the importance of the right assistant — indeed, Graeme Souness had tried to take Smith with him to Liverpool.

Media speculation raged on the likely names: Terry Butcher, Jocky Scott, Bruce Rioch, Ray Wilkins, and even Richard Gough were all mentioned in dispatches. Smith finally plumped for Archie Knox of Manchester United, a close friend since the days when they both played together at Tannadice (indeed they were both in

Mark Hateley, Walter Smith and Chris Woods celebrate Rangers' 41st League Championship triumph.

the Dundee United side which lost 0-3 to Celtic in the 1974 Scottish Cup Final).

Knox came to Ibrox with a formidable reputation as an experienced coach and hard taskmaster.

His playing career had encompassed Forfar Athletic, St. Mirren and Dundee United, before returning to Station Park as player manager. From there he moved on to Aberdeen as assistant to Alex Ferguson, before taking charge of Dundee for two-and-a-half seasons, then resigning to rejoin 'Fergie' as co-manager at Pittodrie.

In 1986, both men moved to Old Trafford, and it is surely as clear an indication as any that Rangers can now compete with the best and biggest clubs in England, that Knox jumped at the chance to move to Ibrox.

Knox, like Smith, is a man with a track record in management. He had come perilously close to taking Dundee, with very limited resources, into Europe; he had tasted F.A. Cup success at Wembley with Manchester United and before

joining Rangers, had helped to take the Old Trafford men to the brink of European success.

Perhaps his greatest achievement, however, lay in the humble surroundings of Station Park, Forfar, where he built a very modest club into one capable of holding its own in the Scottish First Division, and which under his control in season 1977/78, took Rangers to the very brink of defeat in the League Cup semi-final at Hampden. A late Derek Parlane equaliser saved Rangers (who went on to win the treble that season) from a defeat of Berwick proportions.

For the second member of his backroom team Walter Smith used the Tannadice connection yet again, appointing Billy Kirkwood in May 1991. On the coaching staff at Dundee, Kirkwood had, of course, made his name as a player at Dundee United from 1976-1988, before going on to play for both Dunfermline Athletic and Dundee.

So the "Changes at the Top" were now complete and the new management team installed, an exciting combination of skills to confront the challenge of a new season.

TRIUMPH AND TRAGEDY

A season that would ultimately climax in one of the most dramatic days in Scottish football history began calmly enough.

Rangers set off on July 22nd for Italy and the Il Ciocco training camp high in the Tuscany Hills, with new signing Mark Hateley from Monaco in the squad.

A week's training, and Rangers are ready for the off! As always, manager Graeme Souness stresses that the League Championship is his No 1 priority.

Pre-season friendlies at Lesser Hampden and Dens Park against Queen's Park and Dundee are both noteworthy. The 1-0 win at Mount Florida features Australian Paul Trimboli and Dutchman Pieter Huistra in the line-up (the latter is signed from Twente Enschede for a £300,000 fee) and the 2-2 draw in the 'City of Discovery' marks Graeme Souness's final game in light blue. He scores with a 25-yarder!

The other goalscorer, incidentally, is Mark Hateley with his first goal for the club.

And so it's on to Ibrox, with two prestige friendlies against Dinamo Kiev and Manchester United. Rangers fans receive a foretaste of the shape of things to come, as Oleg Kuznetsov scores in just two minutes, and the Soviets go on to win 3-1. Rangers have already secured Kuznetsov's transfer at the end of the Soviet season (October).

Gary Stevens and Trevor Steven return for the Kiev match, having been given extended leave of absence after their exertions in the World Cup. Chris Woods joins them for the game against the 'Red Devils' on 15th August, but Mark Walters misses a penalty, and Russell Beardsmore nets a late winner for United.

Two defeats are never easy to take, even in friendlies, but what is totally unacceptable is the abuse directed at Mark Hateley for no apparent

reason. Graeme Souness slams the minority of fans involved, and receives the support of all true Rangers followers.

Terry Butcher joins his colleagues for the John McNeill Testimonial at Greenock two days later, where Rangers win 4-0, with John Spencer, newly returned from Hong Kong, scoring twice. Many observers wonder whether the Rangers captain has come back from a cartilage operation too soon.

The Scottish League Centenary match at Hampden sees Gary Stevens captain the League to a 1-0 win over Scotland — Stuart Munro and Ally McCoist are on the losing side!

The Season Starts

Competitive football returns at last. Rangers opening fixture is a League Cup tie at home to 2nd Division East Stirling. 25,595 watch as Rangers coast to a 5-0 triumph, Mark Hateley answering the critics with two goals, and keeping Ally McCoist on the bench — the first of many such occasions.

The league season opens on August 25th, and as the Championship flag is unfurled, Rangers fans dream of a third successive title for the first time since World War II.

Rangers take an early lead against Dunfermline in an entertaining game. Hateley heads home a John Brown cross in ten minutes but ex-Ranger Ian McCall levels matters within six minutes. The Light Blues press incessantly, but not until the 74th minute do they regain the lead, when Maurice Johnston heads home a Mark Walters cross, and within 60 seconds Walters himself converts a penalty after being fouled.

First Division Kilmarnock are the next opponents in the Skol League Cup, and a certain Terry Hurlock, a £300,000 signing from Millwall Athletic makes his debut in this match, quickly endearing himself to the fans. The Ayrshire team is packed full of experience, including ex-Ranger Dave McKinnon, and it takes the Ibrox men all of 73 minutes to break the deadlock, when a Hurlock rocket is parried by Bobby Geddes, allowing Johnston to fire home.

Left, above: Terry Hurlock clashes with Derek Whyte in the first 'Old Firm' game of the season, while Gary Stevens, Nigel Spackman and John Collins look on. Below: A big grin for the cameras as Ally McCoist marks yet another goal, against St Mirren this time.

TRIUMPH AND TRAGEDY

September — Into Europe

Rangers drop their first league point in a disappointing goalless draw at Easter Road on September 1st, but soon make up for the lack of goals by scoring six against Raith Rovers three days later. Ally, Mark and Mo all start this game, and 'Super-Ally' hits a hat-trick after the Fifers had had the audacity to actually take the lead!

Terry Butcher will remember this one as well — he scores at either end! First of all, he heads a Gordon Dalziel cross cleanly past Chris Woods, then goes straight up the park to crash a thunderous 30-yard shot into the top corner of the net.

Rangers visit Edinburgh for the second successive Saturday and play well to win 3-1, with Ally McCoist netting two. Pieter Huistra notches his first league goal, in a match where the result costs Hearts manager Alex MacDonald his job.

Richard Gough keeps his eye on the ball.

The first mid-week international of season 1990/91 finds Ally McCoist scoring the winner for Scotland at Hampden in a 2-1 European Championship win over Romania, Chris Woods in goal for England at Wembley as Hungary are defeated 1-0 in a friendly before an incredible 51,459 and Chris Vinnicombe making his England under-21 debut against the same opposition at Southampton, England winning 3-1.

Meanwhile, John Spencer signs a new two-year contract just two days after scoring four goals at Firs Park in a friendly against East Stirling, and one day after his 20th birthday.

The first 'Old Firm' game of the new season is held at Ibrox on September 15th. A full-house of 38,543 see Rangers dominant for almost the entire match, as they totally outplay their opponents, only for Pat Bonner to defy the odds in a display of goalkeeping seldom bettered.

Almost inevitably, it is Celtic who take the lead in 53 minutes when, in virtually their first attack of the entire match, Derek Whyte heads home a John Collins free-kick.

Unbelievable as it seems, Rangers are now behind and for some time thereafter seem to lose their collective way, until Terry Hurlock, on his 'Old Firm' debut, scores with a low shot from 25 yards in 65 minutes.

The match concludes as it began, with Rangers attacking incessantly, and Celtic hanging on grimly for a 1-1 draw.

The reserve team, however, did secure an 'Old Firm' victory that day — 3-2 at Celtic Park in the Premier Reserve League after leading 3-0 at the interval. This was their second win over Celtic so early in the season, having already triumphed 2-0 at Shotts in the Reserve League West.

The sun-kissed Island of Malta is the setting for Rangers' twelfth entry into the European Cup. The opposition is hardly the most difficult, but conditions are in many ways a great leveller, with a badly rutted pitch and soaring temperatures.

The George Cross island is set alight, however, as the Light Blues score an emphatic 4-0 victory watched by a large contingent of Rangers fans in the 4,000 crowd. An early penalty score by Ally McCoist, after the Ranger had been fouled by goalkeeper Camilleri, settles the nerves; but Rangers are facing opponents who seldom venture across the halfway line and it is the hour-mark before the Ibrox men add a second,

Above: Mark Walters in full flow — a superb sight. Tommy Wilson of Dunfermline gives chase. Below: It's there! Johnston celebrates as John Brown tucks the ball away against Motherwell.

TRIUMPH AND TRAGEDY

when a McCoist pass releases Hateley, who nets with ease.

Two late Maurice Johnston goals give the scoreline a comfortable look and Rangers have every reason to be satisfied with their lot. Mark Walters, however, has good reason to feel aggrieved, having been booked for taking a free-kick too quickly!

Rangers return to Scotland in ample time for the difficult trip to Tannadice Park, Dundee and could hardly have got off to a better start, when a Huistra/Steven move enables Johnston to net from close range.

Rangers are well on top in the early stages of the match, with Pieter Huistra in outstanding form, but a rash tackle by Jim McInally on the 'Flying Dutchman' puts paid to that danger, and earns the ex-Celt the first of what would be four cautions he would receive in matches against Rangers during the course of the season.

The turning point of the game undoubtedly arrives in the 38th minute, when a long kick-out from Billy Thomson is spectacularly headed into his own net from fully 25 yards by Terry Butcher. Billy McKinlay notches a late winner for United.

There is, however, no time to regret Rangers' first competitive defeat of the season, as Aberdeen await at Hampden Park in the semi-final of the League Cup.

The major talking point of the evening is the omission of Terry Butcher (as events will turn out, he has played his last first-team game for the club); but it is another Englishman, Trevor Steven, who is the outstanding player afield, with a superb display, culminating in the scoring of a magnificent goal on the half-hour mark when he sweeps through the Aberdeen defence with great control to steer the ball past Theo Snelders.

Thus the holders are out. Rangers have gained ample revenge for the Final defeat of the previous season and now face Celtic, the Parkhead men having defeated Dundee United 2-0 in the other semi.

Motherwell are never the easiest opponents, nor the most popular visitors to Ibrox and so it proves three days later, when it takes the introduction of substitute Mark Hateley to turn the game Rangers' way. John Brown scores the solitary goal in the 48th minute.

Terry Hurlock, in the thick of it as usual.

October — Hampden Triumph

Dreich conditions and torrential rain greet Rangers' Maltese visitors for the return leg of the European Cup tie on the night of 2nd October, the weather and live television coverage restricting the attendance to just 20,627.

Early goals from David Dodds and John Spencer (on his European debut) kill the tie stone-dead and the game will be remembered more than anything else for Chris Woods' second-half penalty miss and for Maurice Johnston's first ever hat-trick for Rangers.

If anything, the weather is even worse the following Saturday as Rangers travel north to Aberdeen. Incessant rain has turned the pitch into something akin to a lake and there are few apart from referee Les Mottram who think that the game should go ahead.

Nevertheless, Rangers are happy to depart with a goalless draw, although the conditions lead directly to a tragic accident, when Theo Snelders suffers a depressed fracture of the cheekbone following a collision with Ally McCoist.

16

One of the early season talking points: Trevor Steven is fouled on the edge of the Celtic box.

The next day, Ally is involved in a happier event, when he marries girlfriend Allison Mitchell at Whitburn Parish Church, near Sunderland.

The long-awaited arrival of Soviet star Oleg Kuznetsov finally happens — the 27-year old World Cup star, a £1.2 million signing from Dinamo Kiev (where he won a European Cup Winners Cup medal in 1986) has helped his club to win their League Championship and therefore is able to arrive earlier than expected. Capped more than fifty times for the USSR, Oleg's debut coincides with arguably Rangers' finest display of the season — a 5-0 mauling of St. Mirren at Ibrox before 38,031 spectators, as Rangers turn on a superb display of football, with the Ukrainian demonstrating his class time and time again and goals from Ally McCoist (2), Mark Walters (2) and Maurice Johnston the icing on the cake.

The league title race is now taking shape after eight games, with Dundee United in pole position with 13 points, two clear of Rangers, three of Aberdeen and four ahead of Celtic. For the reserves, Rangers lie in fifth place in the Premier Reserve League with seven points from five games — five points adrift of Dundee United and four of Celtic, both of whom have played three games more. In the Reserve League West, Rangers lie second, with ten points from six games — one point behind Clydebank.

On Monday, 15th October, Rangers visit Tyneside for the first time since 1969, playing a friendly at the magnificent Gateshead International Stadium, where a young Rangers team defeats the Vauxhall Conference side 2-1, Paul Willis and Craig Lewis being the goalscorers, in front of a remarkable attendance that must have been close to 4,000.

Two days later, Ally McCoist misses a penalty as Scotland defeat Switzerland 2-1 at Hampden in the European Championship, whilst at Wembley, Chris Woods keeps another clean sheet as England open their European campaign with a 2-0 win over Poland. Chris Vinnicombe, meanwhile, plays at White Hart Lane for England's under-21 team, who go down 1-0 to Poland.

Rangers pay their first-ever visit to McDiarmid Park, Perth on October 20th, attracting a record attendance of 10,504 to the model ground. Admission charges of up to £10 and car-parking fees of £5 anger Rangers fans; but the club, too, have to pay a heavy price as Oleg Kuznetsov is carried off after 18 minutes with a knee injury — he will require surgery and play no further part in Rangers' season. On the field of play, Rangers are rather lucky to escape with a goalless draw.

TRIUMPH AND TRAGEDY

Rangers' European Cup second round opponents are the redoubtable Red Star Belgrade (Crevna Zvezda Beograd) and a massive attendance in excess of 80,000 pack the Red Star Stadium to witness the first leg.

Rangers are severely handicapped as are British clubs in general (given that each home country is treated separately) by the UEFA ruling limiting 16-man squads to four non-nationals.

In the cauldron that is the oval bowl of the 'Maracana', Rangers are torn apart by a superb display of attacking football from the Yugoslav champions. The pace, skill and control of front men Prosinecki, Pancev, and Binic create gaps in the light blue defence time and time again.

The speed of full-back Radinovic creates the opening goal, his cross from the right wing being diverted into his own net by John Brown after just seven minutes.

Somehow, Rangers survive until the 66th minute, when Ian Ferguson concedes a free-kick in a dangerous position with a foul on Stosic. Robert Prosinecki's free-kick finds the net off the upright, with both Chris Woods and the wall found wanting and Rangers are 2-0 down.

In desperate search of the critical away goal, Rangers move forward, and Pieter Huistra misses a golden opportunity when it seems easier to score, only for Red Star to sweep upfield on the counter-attack in a lightning move which ends with Darko Pancev scoring an opportunist goal.

Rangers have a mountain to climb for the second leg and the Rangers fans inside the Red Star Stadium know that the European Cup dream has ended for another season.

"We were lucky to lose only three goals," states Graeme Souness and few would disagree.

Rangers now have to pick themselves up for the League Cup Final at Hampden Park just four days later, with Maurice Johnston absent due to an injury picked up in the opening minute of the Belgrade tie; but the Light Blues defy the odds by coming from behind to win 2-1 after Paul Elliott has given Celtic the lead, goals by Mark Walters and Richard Gough taking the trophy to Ibrox for a record 17th time before 62,817 spectators.

It's that man again. . . Hurlock, Spackman and McCoist celebrate another goal by 'Super Ally', against Hearts.

TRIUMPH AND TRAGEDY

November — Exit Europe

Hibernian are the Ibrox visitors on November 3rd as Rangers turn in a devastating first-half display to lead 4-0 through goals by Mark Hateley (2), Mark Walters and Trevor Steven and then coast through the second-half, leaving

us to ponder how Hibs managed to hold Rangers to a draw on September 1st.

Tuesday, November 6th sees Rangers knocked out of the BP Youth Cup 2-3 at Hamilton and 24 hours later, the chances of overcoming the 3-0 deficit to Red Star Belgrade is reflected in the attendance of 23,821 at Ibrox for the return leg. The Slavs control the game with an impressive display, taking the lead when Darko Pancev volleys the ball home in the 51st minute.

Rangers equalise in 76 minutes when McCoist heads home from a Spackman cross. Ally hits the post soon afterwards from a Walters cross, then misses an open goal, but the game finishes 1-1 and Rangers are left with further injury problems, Richard Gough having suffered a chest injury.

One consolation is the performance of young Sandy Robertson, whose skill shines like a beacon in the second-half.

Red Star Belgrade will, as events unfold, go on to eliminate Dinamo Dresden and Bayern

Nigel Spackman and Dave Bowman in a mid-air duel last November.

Munich before defeating Olympique Marseilles in a penalty shoot-out in Bari to capture the European Cup after a dreadful final.

It is worthy of note that in their successful European campaign, Red Star won every away match except the one at Ibrox!

Three days later, Rangers' cup of woe is overflowing when Dundee United complete a league double with another 2-1 win at Ibrox, a smash and grab act if ever there was one. Rangers, despite losing Trevor Steven after just seven minutes with hamstring trouble, lay siege to the United goal for almost the entire game, but twice lose goals to Darren Jackson in breakaways, with Ally McCoist the lone Rangers marksman, although he earlier missed a penalty.

That same day at Tannadice, Terry Butcher plays his final game in a Rangers jersey, Dundee United winning 1-0 in a Premier Reserve League fixture. The following day Rangers' youth team get off to a winning start in their Glasgow Cup campaign, defeating Clyde 5-0 at Baillieston.

Terry Butcher is appointed player-manager of Coventry City on Wednesday, November 14th; on the same day Ally McCoist nets Scotland's

*Left: Take that,
Packie! McCoist
exults, Bonner
despairs as the ball
goes into the Celtic
net. Below: John
Brown tests St
Johnstone keeper
Lindsay Hamilton.
Mark Hateley waits
for the rebound.*

TRIUMPH AND TRAGEDY

goal in Sofia in the 1-1 draw with Bulgaria and Chris Woods keeps goal in Dublin as England draw 1-1 with Eire. Chris Vinnicombe is more successful — the under-21 side defeating their Irish counterparts in Cork 3-0.

Rangers welcome back Maurice Johnston (and have David Dodds in central defence) as they feature in a six-goal thriller at Fir Park on November 17th. Leading 1-0 from early on thanks to a Mark Walters 20-yarder, ex-Ranger Davie Cooper lights the fuse with a free-kick in the 73rd minute, only for Rangers to respond immediately with goals from Maurice Johnston and Gary Stevens, the latter a superb chip. Steve Bryce adds a second for the home team with five minutes left to ensure a thrilling climax, but a

swift breakaway on the final whistle enables Gary Stevens to net his second, the first time he has done so in seven years!

The following day, Rangers' youth team miss innumerable chances, including one from the penalty spot, in a 1-3 defeat by Celtic at Kirkintilloch.

An early Mark Hateley goal secures two points at Dunfermline on Tuesday, November 20th and this is followed by a joyous weekend for Rangers fans — the weekend of the "Double

Maurice Johnston celebrates his goal against Celtic. Note the cycle shorts!

A spectacular Johnston strike against Motherwell is admiringly watched by John Brown and Mark Walters.

Two" — as first of all a Premier Reserve League fixture at Ibrox sees Rangers comfortably defeat Celtic 2-0 with goals from David Hagen and Gary McSwegan, to be followed 24 hours later by a 2-1 victory at Celtic Park.

Rangers go into that Parkhead fixture minus Gough, Kuznetsov, Steven and Durrant, yet still win at the home of their greatest rivals.

The young Sandy Robertson plays a prominent role in midfield and it falls to Maurice Johnston to notch his first goal at his old haunt in just 8 minutes to see Rangers off to a real flier. A Paul Elliott header just six minutes before the break levels matters and when Rangers lose Johnston through illness just after the interval things don't look too good. However, 'super-sub' Ally McCoist nets a memorable winner five minutes later, being released by Terry Hurlock following a powerful, but fair, challenge in midfield and totally wrong-footing Pat Bonner — Ally's 'dance of delight' says it all!

That victory takes Rangers to the top of the Premier Division, ahead of Aberdeen on goal difference, with Dundee United one point adrift and Celtic trailing by a full six points. The Premier Reserve League shows Rangers second to Celtic by just one goal, with Dundee United again just one point behind.

The only blot on a wonderful weekend is the news that Rangers' youth team have gone down 1-2 to Partick Thistle at Kirkintilloch.

The delights of playing football in Scotland . . . Gary Stevens and Pieter Van de Ven splash out at Pittodrie, while Sandy Robertson and Dundee United's Christian Dailly struggle in the snow.

TRIUMPH AND TRAGEDY

December — Goals Galore

Joe Jordan's first visit to Ibrox as Hearts' manager on the first day of December results in a 4-0 Rangers romp, with Sandy Robertson, Terry Hurlock and Mark Walters outstanding, the goalscorers being Johnston, Hurlock, McCoist and Walters. The next day, Rangers travel to New Cumnock to play Glenafton Athletic in a benefit match for four young Rangers fans killed in a road accident on their way to Tannadice in September — Gary McSwegan scores both goals as Rangers win 2-0.

Meanwhile, Rangers announce that they have turned down invitations to play in both the Tennent's Sixes, and a similar tournament in Paris.

Four more goals are recorded on December 8th as St. Johnstone are readily despatched, with Trevor Steven welcomed back after injury. Mark Walters (2), Maurice Johnston and Gary Stevens are the net-finders.

Australian youngster Craig Lewis scores four himself the very next day, as Rangers Youths rout Queen's Park 6-0 at Baillieston — but it is not enough to stop Celtic and Partick Thistle qualifying for the Glasgow Cup Final.

"The Rangers Roadshow" — a series of video/ chat evenings to meet the fans in towns around Scotland — is unveiled by Public Relations Executive, John Greig and Rangers also announce that they have purchased the lease of Moore Park, the home of Junior club St. Anthony's, with the intention being that reserve and third eleven fixtures would be played there. The ground will be renamed Struth Park and in time it is the intention to build a grandstand there and to install undersoil heating.

Club Captain Richard Gough is welcomed back at Paisley one week later, having missed six games, as Rangers secure a comfortable 3-0 triumph, with Mark Hateley in outstanding form. He lays on the first for Mark Walters in eight minutes, is barged in the back by Tom Black for the penalty which Maurice Johnston converts for the second in 70 minutes, then heads a fine third just eight minutes from the end to clinch victory.

Rangers, meanwhile, put forward proposals to UEFA suggesting a change in the format of the European Cup, introducing two groups of four clubs at the quarter-final stage, instead of the present knock-out system. The idea is later accepted by the governing body for implementation from season 1991/92.

Rangers reach "Seventh Heaven" in a Reserve League West fixture at Celtic Park on Wednesday, December 19th — defeating their great rivals 7-4, with hat-tricks from both John Spencer and Gary McSwegan. Indeed, the Light Blues are 7-1 ahead with 25 minutes to go and looking likely to score every time they cross the halfway line, so devastating and rampant are their attacks — and yet . . . slackness creeps in, the players ease off the accelerator and Celtic score three times in the closing stages to make the scoreline more respectable.

Aberdeen are the pre-Xmas visitors to Ibrox on December 22nd with Nigel Spackman absent through illness. Rangers are hit by a further blow when Trevor Steven suffers a recurrence of his hamstring injury in just ten minutes. An evenly-balanced game explodes with the goal of the season in 61 minutes, when Ally McCoist controls a Gary Stevens throw-in on his chest, wheels and volleys an unstoppable 20-yard shot into the roof of the net.

Ten minutes later, another superb goal as McCoist sweeps home a Huistra cross and Rangers seem home and dry; but Aberdeen strike back within minutes with a Jim Bett penalty and the game is once again in the melting pot.

In the closing stages, Rangers are denied two strong penalty claims, but it is ex-Ranger Bett who shoots home through a crowded penalty area to level matters in the final minute.

Aberdeen are still alive in the title race!

Rangers have more success at Pittodrie, where John Spencer scores four more goals as Rangers rout Aberdeen 6-1 in the Premier Reserve League.

The New Year holiday programme is always a critical time for football clubs and Rangers show their championship mettle with three straight wins against quality opposition.

Tannadice Park is the setting on December 29th, with United having already defeated Rangers twice this season. An early goal from Darren Jackson looks ominous on a day of snowstorms but Maurice Johnston soon equalises. Mark Walters nets a stunning winner before the interval, ghosting past three defenders before curling the ball into the roof of the net from the edge of the box.

Our review of season 1990/91 continues on page 32.

BOB McPHAIL

THE term 'living legend' is too often over-worked and misused, but if ever the description was applicable, then it is surely in the instance of Bob McPhail.

Born on 25th October 1905, in Barrhead, 'Greetin' Boab' as he became widely known, is the last link with a different era — the last of the many great players who played with Hughie Gallacher, Alan Morton and David Meiklejohn. He played in the historic 1928 Scottish Cup Final and in the tragic 'Old Firm' encounter of September 1931 at Ibrox when Celtic goalkeeper John Thomson suffered his fatal injury.

A career that started with Braehead Ashgrove, moved on to Pollok Juniors, Arthurlie (for one game only) and then to the ranks of the seniors, with Airdrieonians. Bob signed for the Lanarkshire club on Christmas Day 1923 for a fee of £20, with the promise of weekly wages of £3 per week in the reserves, £5 in the first team, and £1 win bonus.

These sums were riches indeed for an apprentice moulder earning 17/9d (89p) a week and within three months, McPhail was making his first-team debut for Airdrie in a Scottish Cup tie against Ayr United — at Ibrox, of all places!

Success came quickly to the young McPhail — that era was the halcyon time as far as Airdrieonians Football Club were concerned. In four successive years from 1923 they were runners-up in the League Championship and less than one month after his debut, Bob McPhail was a member of the Broomfield side which won the Scottish Cup for the only time in their history, defeating Hibernian 2-0 at Ibrox.

Hughie Gallacher and Bob McPhail were a formidable duo for Airdrie, but in December 1925 Gallacher was transferred to Newcastle United whilst McPhail played at Broomfield for a further 16 months. In all, he scored 74 goals in 109 league games for the Broomfield side.

Transferred to Rangers in April 1927 for the sum of £4,500 after having made his international debut for Scotland against England at Hampden Park just two weeks earlier, Bob quickly established a formidable left-wing partnership with the "Wee Blue Devil", Alan Morton in the great Rangers team of that decade.

Bob's first full season at Ibrox brought Rangers the league and cup double for the first time in their history and McPhail netted Rangers second in the famous 4-0 defeat of Celtic that ended the 25-year Scottish Cup hoodoo.

A strong, bustling inside-forward with a feel for scoring goals, Bob McPhail's Ibrox record speaks for itself — nine League Championship medals, six Scottish Cup, six Charity Cup and five Glasgow Cup, his Scottish Cup career total of seven equalling the 20th-century record of Jimmy McMenemy.

McPhail made exactly 500 appearances for Rangers in all games, scoring 319 goals, his 229 in league games being a club record if one discounts the wartime record of Jimmy Smith.

The outbreak of war in 1939 occurred as McPhail's career was coming to its natural end, but after playing just five more games for Rangers he signed for St Mirren in January 1941, played a few games there, then retired.

Rangers manager Bill Struth asked Bob to look after the reserves — a job he was to hold for the next forty years under five more managers. When asked by the then Chairman, Matt Taylor to join the Board of Directors, he declined the offer, being happy in the role Struth had designated for him.

A life member of Rangers Football Club, his collection of 36 medals adorns the Ibrox Trophy Room.

There can be no doubt that in any Scottish Football Hall of Fame, Bob McPhail merits a special place.

Above: Bob McPhail (right foreground) waits as a high ball comes over during a Rangers-Hearts clash at Ibrox.
Below: Bob's medals on display in the Trophy Room at Ibrox.

The Scottish Cup Final 1981

IT has been ten long years since the Scottish Cup last adorned the Ibrox Trophy Room — ten years in which young Rangers fans have grown up not knowing what it is like to see red, white and blue ribbons attached to the national trophy.

And yet . . . on a summer's evening in May 1981, as Rangers players led by Captain Ally Dawson paraded round Hampden, the light blue legions regarded it as almost an inalienable right that they should be in attendance at the old arena. That final of 1981 was the sixth consecutive such appearance, a run that would finally stretch to a record eight by 1983.

Surprising as it may seem today, Rangers went into that 1981 Final as very much the underdogs — Dundee United had already won the League Cup for the previous two seasons, with Jim McLean having built a formidable side.

Rangers manager John Greig opted for caution in the first game, leaving Davie Cooper and John MacDonald on the substitute's bench, and omitting Derek Johnstone altogether.

The Tannadice men controlled the game from the whistle, with Rangers forced into defence for long periods of the game. An Eamonn Bannon free-kick close to half-time produced a magnificent flying save from Jim Stewart, turning the ball round the post, but clear-cut chances were few and far between. The game gradually developed into a stalemate, until the introduction by John Greig of Davie Cooper and John MacDonald with just ten minutes remaining.

In an inkling, the Light Blues were transformed and Rangers went for the kill. The United goal had several narrow escapes, none more so than when a Cooper cross was guided past McAlpine by MacDonald, only to be headed off the line by David Narey — television evidence was later to prove that MacDonald had in fact used a hand!

The game was in its closing minute when Bobby Russell weaved his way into the penalty area only to be fouled by Iain Phillip. A clear penalty and with it the certain chance to win the Scottish

Cup. The onerous duty of converting it fell to Ian Redford, who had already beaten Hamish McAlpine from the spot in a league game at Ibrox some five weeks earlier; but on this occasion the ball struck the goalkeeper's legs and rebounded to safety.

Extra-time produced no decision and so it was back to Hampden the following Tuesday with John Greig bringing in Dave Cooper, Derek Johnstone and John MacDonald, to the exclusion of Tommy McLean, Colin McAdam and Willie Johnston.

It was a different Rangers altogether that sultry evening. An exciting display of attacking football, orchestrated by the superb skills of Davie Cooper, tore the heart out of the United defence and Rangers took the lead as early as the 10th minute, when Cooper himself took advantage of slack play in the Tannadice ranks to clip the ball home. Ten minutes later it was 2-0 when a Cooper free-kick swung away from the onrushing Johnstone, but fell to Bobby Russell who volleyed the ball into the roof of the net.

At 2-0 ahead Rangers seemed well in command, but three minutes later a certain David Dodds reduced the deficit from a suspiciously offside position. The two-goal margin was restored in 29 minutes when a superb Cooper through-ball released John MacDonald, who placed the ball under McAlpine's body.

The second-half was a formality, with the result sealed in 78 minutes, when MacDonald converted a Redford pass. The 4-1 scoreline was sweet revenge for a similar reversal in an Ibrox league fixture earlier that season, but what no-one could have anticipated amidst the celebrations was that ten years later the next triumph would still be awaited. . . .

Nevertheless, the night was one to be savoured, with Rangers producing their best display of that season and Davie Cooper one of the finest performances of his entire career — a performance which marked him out as, at that time, arguably the best footballer in Britain.

Derek Johnstone turns away in delight as Bobby Russell's super strike puts Rangers 2-0 ahead in the replay. The Cup is on its way to Ibrox!

The Teams

Saturday May 9th 1981

Rangers

Stewart; Jardine, Dawson; Stevens, T. Forsyth, Bett; McLean, Russell, McAdam (Cooper), Redford, W. Johnston (MacDonald).

Dundee United

McAlpine; Holt, Kopel; Phillip (Stark), Hegarty, Narey; Bannon, Milne (Pettigrew), Kirkwood, Sturrock, Dodds.

Tuesday May 12th 1981

Rangers: Cooper, Johnstone and MacDonald for McLean, McAdam and Johnston

Dundee United: Unchanged

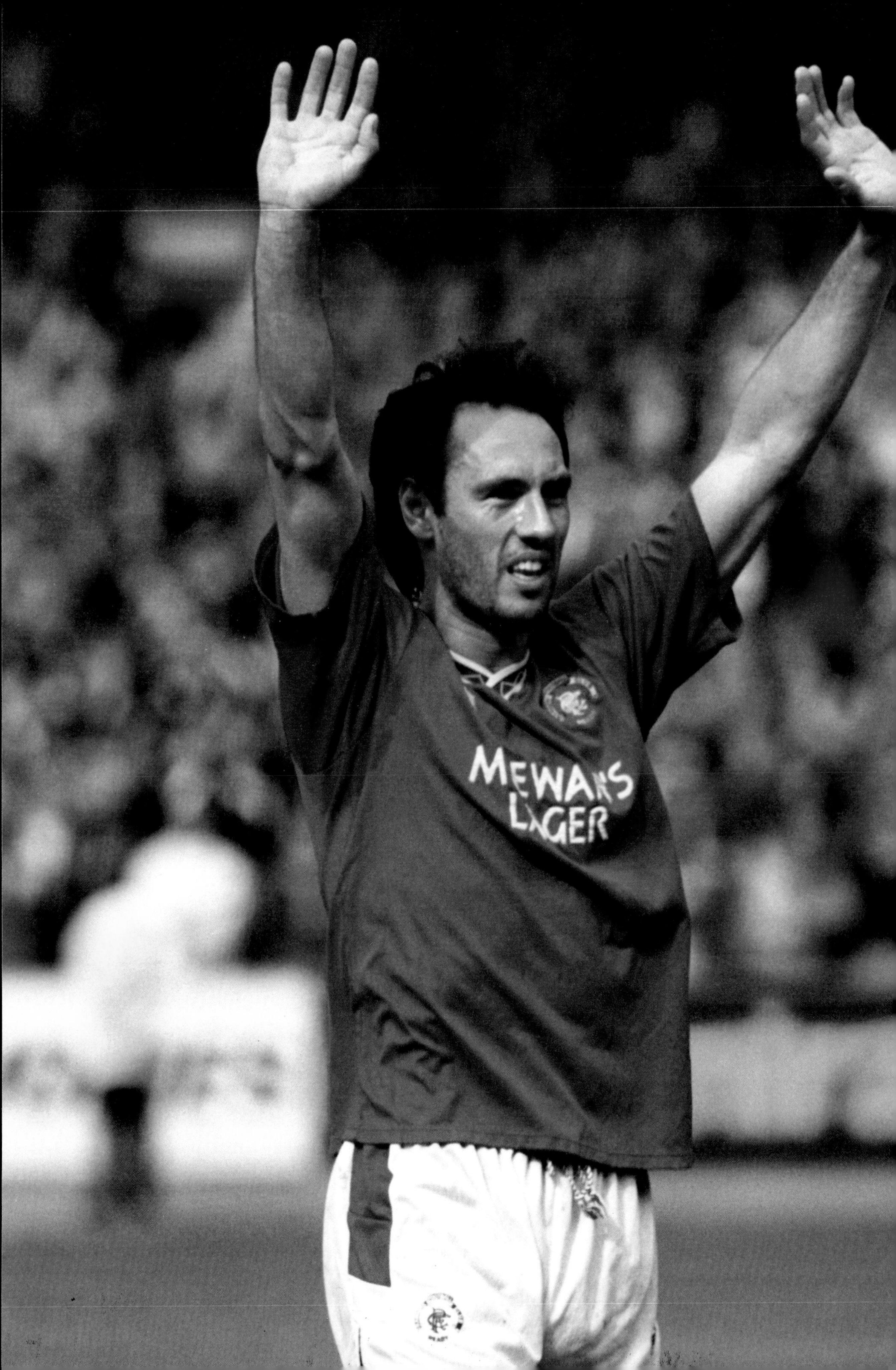

MARK HATELEY

THE story of Mark Hateley's first season as a Ranger was, in the end, one of glorious triumph against overwhelming odds, but it is fair comment that seldom has any Ibrox player had a more difficult introduction to his 'Light Blue' career.

The son of Tony Hateley, who played for Notts County, Aston Villa, Chelsea, Liverpool, Coventry City, Birmingham City and Oldham Athletic, Mark — a much more accomplished player — had been tracked by Graeme Souness for over three years.

Liverpool-born, Mark Hateley's first senior club was Coventry City, with whom he played for five seasons before a big-money transfer to Portsmouth, where 22 league goals in season 1983/84 attracted the interest of A.C. Milan.

A regular first-team player for three seasons at San Siro, Hateley almost signed for Rangers in 1987, and again one year later. By then he had moved on to Monaco, playing alongside Glenn Hoddle. Manager Graeme Souness finally made him a Ranger in July 1990, in a transfer deal conditional on the number of games played during the terms of his four-year contract.

A bustling, powerful striker, whose strongest suit was his aerial threat, Mark had played for England at youth, under-21 and full international level. Even so, his signing was not universally welcomed by Rangers fans, a small minority of whom hurled abuse at him on his Ibrox debut in the pre-season friendly against Dinamo Kiev.

Such disgraceful treatment — almost unprecedented in Rangers' long history — was quite inexplicable and could have broken the spirit of many a footballer; but Hateley showed the strength of character that would serve him so well by buckling down and getting on with the job he was paid to do — score goals!

His first two in light blue came in a 5-0 League Cup trouncing of East Stirling, and were quickly followed by Rangers' opening goal in defence of the League Championship versus Dunfermline Athletic on 25th August 1990. These were the first of fifteen such counters during season 1990/91 — many of them decisive.

The goals were only part of the story, however. It took Mark almost the entire season to win more than grudging acceptance from the light blue legions. Many resented his regular inclusion in the team at the exclusion of the ever-popular Ally McCoist — but that was hardly Hateley's fault! It also had to be appreciated that it took him some time to adapt to the British game again after six years abroad. The more discerning friends of Rangers, however, could recognise a player when they saw one. Bad players do not win 31 full international caps for England, nor do they play three seasons apiece at Milan and Monaco.

The turning-point of the season for Hateley came, perhaps, in the League Cup Final where, although not scoring, he played a pivotal role in the 2-1 defeat of Celtic.

The longer the season went on, the greater became Hateley's contribution, and the more people began to appreciate his contribution to the team. His workrate, distribution, running off the ball, and above all else, of course, his strength in the air were all to prove invaluable for Rangers in the course of the 1990/91 campaign.

True, the goals dried up for Hateley after netting twice in the Scottish Cup tie with Cowdenbeath on 23rd February, but he was hardly alone in that respect. One quite distinct black mark was his ordering-off in the infamous Scottish Cup tie at Celtic Park following an off-the-ball incident with Anton Rogan.

Notwithstanding that dreadful day, and despite the lack of goals, Mark Hateley could hold his head up high as the league season drew to the most dramatic of climaxes.

The final showdown with Aberdeen brought what was surely his finest hour, with the two decisive goals in Rangers' magnificent 2-0 triumph. The first, a stunning 15-yard header from a Mark Walters cross, out-jumping Alex McLeish, was a strike of which Willie Thornton, Jimmy Millar, or Derek Johnstone would have been proud! The second was a real opportunist striker's goal after goalkeeper Michael Watt failed to hold a Maurice Johnston drive.

"There's only one Mark Hateley," sang the light blue legions, and there can surely seldom have been music more sweet to the ears for the English striker.

Truly, the hour had brought forth the man, and Mark Hateley was finally accepted as a Ranger.

RIGHT DOWN TO THE WIRE!

January — Heading for a Record

The traditional New Year's Day fixture with Celtic is scheduled for Ibrox on January 2nd 1991 and a poignant note is struck when Chairman David Murray unveils a plaque to commemorate the 20th Anniversary of the 1971 Ibrox Disaster, when 66 fans lost their lives at the end of the 'Old Firm' game. The one minute's silence is observed by all in the capacity crowd except, sadly, for some in the Broomloan Road Stand.

Rangers win with ease 2-0, Mark Walters

Mark Hateley demonstrates his fearsome aerial power to Hearts defenders Gary Mackay and Craig Levein.

scoring direct from a corner and Mark Hateley adding a second from close range.

Three days later, that man Hateley strikes again, with a late winner at Tynecastle in a game marked by controversial refereeing decisions and stormy weather.

Further injury blows are suffered when it is revealed that both Stuart Munro and Scott Nisbet have had to undergo operations. Nevertheless, Rangers coast to a 2-0 win over Dunfermline at Ibrox on January 12th, with goals from Huistra and Johnston, to chalk up their eleventh consecutive game without defeat, a run which has seen Rangers move five points clear of Aberdeen in the Premier Division and the title race seems a formality — to all but Graeme Souness.

In the Premier Reserve League, Celtic lead with 31 points from 21 games, two clear of Rangers, who have two games in hand and five of Dundee United, who have three in hand. In the Reserve League West, Rangers lie third with 21 points from 14 games, four adrift of both Celtic and Clydebank, but with two games in hand.

Rangers equal the Premier Division record for consecutive away wins with their seventh on the trot at Easter Road, winning 2-0 with consummate ease, in a game remarkable for Maurice Johnston's opening goal incredibly being his last of the season! Meanwhile, Celtic defeat Aberdeen 1-0 at Parkhead to open up a seven-point gap and all of football "knows" that the championship is won and lost!

At Ibrox, an astonishing 10,500 attendance watch as Ian Durrant makes his long-awaited comeback from a horrific knee injury in Rangers' Premier Reserve game with Hibernian, playing the full 90 minutes (as does Trevor Steven) in Rangers' 2-1 win.

Scotland include Nigel Spackman in the squad to face the USSR at Ibrox on 6th February, on the strength of his grandfather being born in Prestonpans; but within 24 hours Nigel is withdrawn as it is realised that his inclusion contravenes a private agreement between the four Home International countries.

Continued on page 36.

Above: Pieter Huistra nods home for Rangers' third against Dunfermline in January. Below: Trevor Steven gets in a strike during the cup-tie against Cowdenbeath.

Pieter Huistra acrobatically beats Hibs' Willie Orr and closes in on Andy Goram.

RIGHT DOWN TO THE WIRE

Rangers' quest for their first Scottish Cup success in ten years is delayed until Tuesday January 29th, due to the demands of satellite television. No matter, Rangers defeat Dunfermline by the same score (and just as easily) as in their recent league meeting, Huistra and Spackman being the goalscorers.

Friday January 31st sees the Scottish League clubs vote for a reconstruction proposal introducing a 12-team, 44-game Premier Division next season, with Rangers and the other major clubs dissenting.

On the same day, Trevor Steven and Scott Nisbet escape serious injury in a car crash.

February — The Shut-out Kings

A late postponement due to severe frost takes care of Rangers' visit to McDiarmid Park on February 2nd, but the Ibrox players are in demand the following midweek for international duty.

Richard Gough captains Scotland — the first Rangers players to do so since Graeme Souness — and Ally McCoist also plays in the first full international match to be held at Ibrox Stadium for more than fifty years. In front of 20,763 fans, Scotland lose 0-1 to a last-minute USSR goal.

Meanwhile Trevor Steven plays at Wembley as England defeat Cameroon 2-0 in a friendly international, thanks to two Gary Lineker goals, before a 61,075 attendance and in Swansea, Mark Walters makes his senior representative debut in a 'B' international, as England beat Wales 1-0.

Saturday, February 9th finds John Spencer deservedly making his league debut, with Mark Hateley and Maurice Johnston sidelined through illness. 'Spennie' has a hand in a poor game's only goal, a volley from Ally McCoist in 53 minutes.

Maurice Johnston, meanwhile, reconsiders his decision never to play for Scotland again and is welcomed back into the fold by manager Andy Roxburgh — a move which generates considerable controversy!

Johnston is on the bench and is not needed, as Rangers win 2-0 at home to Motherwell on February 16th, with two spectacular goals (chips from the edge of the area) from McCoist and Hateley.

Rangers still lead Aberdeen by seven clear points with eleven games remaining in the Premier Division, whilst, in the Premier Reserve

League, trailing Celtic by nine points (but with six games in hand) and in the Reserve League West lying three and two points respectively behind Clydebank and Celtic, but with two games in hand over each.

The quest for the Premier Reserve League suffers a body blow on February 22nd when Rangers, leading 2-1 at Love Street with 20 minutes remaining, see Sandy Robertson miss a penalty. Thomas Stickroth equalises within the minute and John Spencer is ordered-off — a vital point lost.

The next day, Rangers coast to a 5-0 Scottish Cup fourth round victory over Cowdenbeath and then find that lightning does indeed strike twice — the quarter-final draw sends Rangers to Celtic Park again!

Manager Graeme Souness pledges his future to Rangers in answer to speculation linking him with the Liverpool post sensationally vacated days earlier by Kenny Dalglish . . . .

Rangers are fined £23,000 by the SFA for the omission of an advertisement for Scottish Cup sponsors, Tennent's Lager, from the Dunfermline programme of January 29th.

The trip to McDiarmid Park, Perth, on Tuesday, February 26th is potentially a record-breaking

Nigel Spackman motors past Gary Mackay of Hearts

Above: Ian Ferguson takes on Hearts' John Robertson as Hurlock and Gough look anxiously on. Below: Maurice Johnston rises to the occasion while a Dunfermline defender tests the quality of Ally McCoist's jersey.

RIGHT DOWN TO THE WIRE

one, with Rangers poised to secure their eighth consecutive away league victory. The Light Blues are denied this feat by some questionable refereeing decisions on the part of Sandy Roy of Aberdeen, who denies Rangers two penalty claims in a 1-1 draw. Pieter Huistra heads a late equaliser after Allan Moore has given 'Saints' the lead very much against the run of play — the first goal Rangers have conceded all year (encompassing eight games).

March — The Dam Bursts

The loss of a single point is hardly catastrophic — but Rangers are again frustrated by events when visiting Pittodrie the following Saturday. Having had the better of the play for much of the game, Rangers spurn a late chance when Maurice Johnston heads high and wide from close in and watch horrified as Hans Gillhaus sweeps the ball home in the last minute following a free-kick taken from the wrong place. Rangers first defeat since 10th November 1990 — 17 games unbeaten!

Suddenly, Aberdeen are only four points adrift following a midweek 2-0 win at Motherwell with nine games remaining . . .

That same day, March 2nd, Aberdeen also score in the last minute at Ibrox to secure a 2-2 result and rob Rangers of a vital point in the Premier Reserve League.

Rangers steady the boat on March 9th with a 2-1 home win over Hearts before 36,128 spectators. Trevor Steven opens the scoring with a superb left-foot volley in 17 minutes, only for ex-Ranger Derek Ferguson to equalise twelve minutes later, but a piece of Mark Walters magic provides the winner on the hour.

Aberdeen drop what seems to be a crucial point in a 0-0 draw at home to Dunfermline on Wednesday, March 13th, to leave Rangers five points clear with eight games remaining. That same night, Rangers Reserves win 4-0 against Clyde at Linlithgow in a League Cup tie. Sandy Robertson, Gary McSwegan, John Morrow and Ian Durrant are the goalscorers.

Chris Woods bravely holds off a high challenge.

Another Johnston special on its way as Mo powers a great header into the net against Dunfermline.

Not this time . . . Ally's header just missed the net in the March 'Old Firm' game, to the relief of Paul Elliott and Pat Bonner.

Rangers' world collapses about them on Sunday, March 17th at Celtic Park as they lose 0-2 to Celtic in the Scottish Cup. The omens are not good before the match, with Nigel Spackman and John Brown absent through injury and Ally McCoist absent because he spent two days at Cheltenham races! Graeme Souness also raises a few eyebrows with his team selection and tactics — the inclusion of Stuart Munro and Ian Ferguson, both long-term injury absentees, is surely questionable given the importance of the game.

An early Gerry Creaney goal, volleying home a Coyne header, suggests that Rangers' Scottish Cup jinx is not about to end and in 13 minutes Rangers suffer a severe loss when Trevor Steven is carried off with a damaged knee, which will keep him out for the rest of the season. Deeper gloom descends when Terry Hurlock deflects a Dariusz Wdowczyk free-kick high past Chris Woods, leaving Rangers with the proverbial mountain to climb.

However, second half mayhem sees Terry Hurlock, Mark Walters and Mark Hateley ordered off, together with Celtic's Peter Grant.

Afterwards Graeme Souness apologises for his team's lack of discipline — but one is left to ponder why a side with the best disciplinary record in the country over the past two-and-a-half years are suddenly involved in such a debacle.

Nevertheless, Celtic are through to the Scottish Cup semi-finals, where they will lose 2-4 to Motherwell in the replay of a 0-0 draw, the Fir Park men going on to lift the national trophy in a thrilling final against Dundee United.

Young midfielder Shaun Rouse is given a boost when he is called into the England under-19 squad on a four-day trip to Trinidad and Tobago.

Rangers are, of course, endeavouring to win three league titles this season and a 6-1 win at Ayr on March 20th is a vital step towards the Reserve League West Championship; but three days later, a vital point is lost in a goalless draw at home to Dundee United in the Premier Reserve League, requiring Rangers to win their final three games by eight goals in total to pip Celtic, who have completed their programme.

Aberdeen, meanwhile, have secured a crucial 2-1 win at Tannadice to put the pressure firmly on the champions, who pay their second consecutive Sunday call to the East End of Glasgow, where it is, alas, like watching a re-run of a bad movie as Rangers slump to a 0-3 defeat.

The Light Blues are without the suspended Hurlock, Walters and Hateley, as well as all their injury problems, but welcome back Spackman and McCoist.

Rangers actually play much better than the previous week, but the rub of the green eludes them at critical phases during the match, with John Spencer in particular missing two golden opportunities and Scott Nisbet perhaps unlucky to be sent off.

Rangers now lead Aberdeen by three points, with seven games remaining. Meanwhile, the Ibrox men are invited to participate in the prestigious Makita Tournament at Wembley Stadium in August, but sadly the plan falls through in the course of time for various reasons and Rangers are denied the honour of being the first Scots club to play at the Empire Stadium.

Richard Gough and Ally McCoist are in the Scottish team which draws 1-1 with Bulgaria at Hampden in the European Championship on 27th March, but Ally suffers a groin injury which will keep him out until the closing moments of the season. Down south, Chris Vinnicombe captains England's under-21's to a 3-1 win over Eire at Brentford.

New signing Brian Reid (£300,000 from Morton) makes his debut at East End Park, Dunfermline, on March 30th in a game marked by yet more controversy. Ian Ferguson is ordered off and the decision seems so harsh that even Dunfermline players appeal to the referee's better nature! Rangers are nevertheless inspired by the handicap and secure two priceless points when Gary Stevens volleys home from twenty yards after Andy Rhodes has blocked a Mark Hateley effort.

Meanwhile, at Fir Park, Rangers defeat Motherwell 3-1 in the Premier Reserve League, but on the following Wednesday lose 2-0 at Clydebank in a crucial Reserve League West fixture and now trail the 'Bankies' by six points and Celtic by seven, although having three and four games in hand respectively.

April — The Prodigal Returns

Ian Durrant makes his long-awaited return to the Rangers first-team at Ibrox Stadium on April 6th against Hibernian, and plays the full 90 minutes. Rangers drop a critical point in a goalless draw, with Andy Goram producing superb saves from both Durrant and John Spencer. Aberdeen are now only two points and six goals adrift, with five games left.

At Motherwell on the same day, Rangers exit from the Reserve League Cup, beaten 6-5!

Durrant's comeback is capped one week later when he opens the scoring at Ibrox against St. Johnstone in just four minutes, as Rangers welcome back John Brown after a six-week

Rising star. . . John Spencer shows skill, control and determination as he takes on Celtic's big defender, Derek Whyte.

absence through injury, but are without Richard Gough and Mark Walters through suspension and Maurice Johnston through exhaustion!

Durrant's goal, a low 18-yard shot tucked inside Lindsay Hamilton's right-hand post, is followed by John Spencer's first league goal and a late Pieter Huistra counter, but once again Rangers are reduced to ten men, again perhaps a shade unluckily, the helpless victim this time being Brian Reid. Aberdeen, meanwhile, win 4-1 at Tynecastle.

Three days later, Rangers are rocked by the revelation that Graeme Souness is to be the new manager of Liverpool and many friends of Rangers are left to ponder the thoughts and pronouncements of their ex-manager in recent weeks and months.

By the end of the week, Walter Smith has been appointed to succeed Souness. Club Captain, Richard Gough, applauds Smith's elevation, stressing that Smith had been doing most of the work anyway!

Meanwhile, Pieter Huistra plays in Holland's 2-0 win over Finland in Rotterdam in the European Championship.

"Wattie's" baptism as manager is a hectic, hard game at Paisley, won by a spectacular overhead kick from substitute Sandy Robertson just six minutes from time, whilst Aberdeen defeat Motherwell 3-0 at Pittodrie to narrow the gap to four goals and two points. That same afternoon,

Rangers Reserves win 2-1 at home to St. Johnstone in the Premier Reserve League.

On Monday, April 22nd, Rangers pay their first visit to Yorkshire since 1968, going down 1-2 to Northern Premier League side Whitby Town, with youngster James Brown the Ibrox goalscorer.

Rangers home fixture with Dundee United has been brought forward to Wednesday, April 24th courtesy of 'BSkyB' and 32,397 onlookers see the home team win 1-0 thanks to a diving header from Ian Ferguson. The game will be remembered more for the staggering first-half miss by Mark Walters (available again together with Richard Gough) when he turned a Maurice Johnston pass wide of an open goal from a few yards range.

Could the destination of the League Championship yet come down to being decided by one goal, or by that single miss . . . ?

Three days later, Rangers miss out on the Premier Reserve League title by the narrowest of margins possible — on goals scored — having tied with Celtic on both points and goal difference! Needing to defeat Hearts by five clear goals, Rangers win 4-0 thanks to goals from Gary McSwegan (2), Ian Durrant and John Spencer, but at crucial times Pieter Huistra hits the post when it seems easier to score and Neil Murray, clean through, sees his shot hit the legs of Henry Smith. It is not to be . . . .

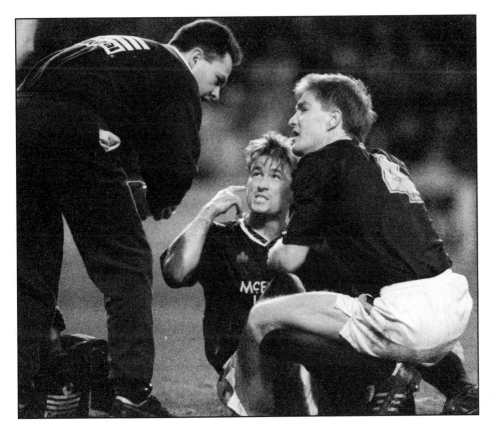

Ouch . . .
Ian Ferguson takes a knock when scoring with a brave diving header against Dundee United. Captain Gough shows concern.

RIGHT DOWN TO THE WIRE

The Reserve League West is still there to be won, however, with Rangers trailing Clydebank by five points and Celtic by three, but with three games in hand over each.

Meanwhile, Aberdeen win 1-0 at Paisley through a late Jim Bett goal to maintain the gap at the top and Archie Knox leaves Manchester United to join Rangers as assistant manager.

May — Simply the Best

Rangers meet disaster at Fir Park, Motherwell on Saturday, May 4th, slumping to a 0-3 defeat in a game that could, and should, have been won. Richard Gough is absent due to illness, later diagnosed as hepatitis and Rangers lose their first goal since Celtic Park in the 25th minute when John Philliben volleys the ball into the roof of the net from fifteen yards.

Almost immediately, the Ibrox men lose Gary Stevens with a thigh injury, but nevertheless press throughout the match, with Ally Maxwell, later to be a Cup Final hero for Motherwell, defying all odds to keep his goal intact.

A golden opportunity presents itself in 73 minutes when Pieter Huistra is fouled, but Mark Walters fails from the penalty spot. There are penalty misses . . . and there are penalty misses . . . but this one soars over by at least five yards!

A superlative Maxwell save from a Hateley header paves the way for the classic sucker punch — and Dougie Arnott supplies it in 85 minutes when he races clear to crash the ball past Chris Woods.

At 2-0, and with the final score from Pittodrie 2-1 to Aberdeen (v St. Johnstone), Rangers would still need only one point in the final showdown with the Dons to clinch the title, but in the closing minutes are caught on the break again by Arnott.

3-0 — the heaviest defeat of the season — and now Rangers must win the crunch match; but there are few who believe they can, with Aberdeen having dropped just one point in their last twelve games.

All is not gloom at Ibrox, however — three Reserve League West games have been won at Greenock, Falkirk and Hamilton and on Wednesday, May 8th, Rangers travel to meet Clyde at Kirkintilloch with the title almost in their grasp, only for Adamslie Park once again to prove a hoodoo ground, with a late goal by substitute Lee Robertson saving a point for Rangers in a 2-2 draw.

It's all down to goal difference again and the thought occurs to many friends of Rangers that three League Championships could actually be lost by such a manner, including two by the number of goals scored!

Grangemouth Athletic's Stadium on the afternoon of Thursday, May 9th is the unlikely setting for the resolution of the Reserve League West and when Falkirk go 2-0 up there seems no way back for the Ibrox men. However, a Gary McSwegan goal on the stroke of half-time makes all the difference and Rangers run riot in the second-half, scoring six goals including four in the last twelve minutes, with hat-tricks from McSwegan and John Morrow.

It was then on to Kilbowie Park, Clydebank, for the last act to be played, with many Rangers players and fans present and the 'Bankies' needing a seven-goal victory margin to take the title. 5-0, however, is the final score against Airdrieonians and Rangers are Reserve League West Champions.

And so, it's right down to the wire — RANGERS v ABERDEEN, MAY 11th 1991 — the Championship crown!

The events of that memorable day are covered in some depth elsewhere in this publication. Suffice to say that two Mark Hateley goals give Rangers a 2-0 win, their 41st League Championship and a third successive title for the first time since the war.

And so, the season ends (though not for everyone) on the most memorable note imaginable. Chris Woods plays in all four of England's tour games in Australia, New Zealand (2) and Malaysia; Mark Walters makes his full England debut on that tour, in Auckland — and Chris Vinnicombe captains England's under-21 side to success in Toulon, France, in a tournament where Brian Reid, John Spencer and Sandy Robertson play for Scotland.

A new era has dawned at Ibrox. Rangers fans are looking forward to 1991/92, anticipating a hopefully injury-free season, some exciting new signings, a fourth consecutive Championship for the first time in over sixty years, the Scottish Cup at last returning to Ibrox, and perhaps even a sustained run in the European Cup!

Perchance to dream . . . .

In the meantime, however, let us savour season 1990/91, when Rangers were 'SIMPLY THE BEST'.

Above: John Spencer almost disappears as team-mates congratulate him on his goal against St Johnstone.
Below: Ally McCoist scoring against Aberdeen in the 2-2 draw.

Rangers v Celtic

September 1977

SEASON 1976/77 had been a barren one for Rangers. The "treble" of 1975/76 was but a fond memory as Rangers slumped badly.

And now came the first 'Old Firm' encounter of season 1977/78. . . .

Saturday, September 10th 1977 was a miserable wet day in Glasgow but it did not deter a crowd of 55,000 from gathering at Ibrox. Neither team had started the new season particularly well. In their opening two league games, Rangers had lost to Aberdeen and Hibernian but had given a

glimmer of hope by beating Partick Thistle 4-0 at Firhill in what was normally a difficult fixture for Rangers. Celtic had opened their campaign by drawing with Dundee United and then losing to Ayr United and Motherwell.

Celtic, the reigning league champions, had a more settled side and most pundits considered them favourites. Rangers, on the other hand, were introducing three players into the 'Old Firm' cauldron for the first time — young Bobby Russell, fresh out of Junior football, Davie Cooper, a £100,000 buy from newly-promoted Clydebank and Gordon Smith, signed from Kilmarnock for £65,000 just over three weeks previously. It was generally accepted that the new Rangers would need time to settle.

Once the match started the early indications seemed to bear this out. Just 18 minutes had elapsed when 'Shuggie' Edvaldsson scored the seemingly vital first goal. The Celtic fans were ecstatic and their cup of joy was running over when the same player knocked in a second goal on the half-hour mark. Rangers were in trouble and their plight was increased when it was discovered that Derek Parlane had broken his jaw, though he bravely played on until the interval.

When the teams re-emerged, Rangers had replaced Parlane with John Greig, playing his first league game of the season after injury. He went into defence, with Derek Johnstone pushed up front into the centre-forward position.

Peter McCloy clutches a cross to thwart 'Shuggie' Edvaldsson, with a young Davie Cooper in the background.

Although two down, Rangers had played a lot of good football, inspired by young Russell and the graceful Gordon Smith and now the presence of Johnstone began to create problems for the Celtic defence. With only eight minutes of the second half played, Gordon Smith smashed home a right foot shot to bring Rangers back into the game. Twelve minutes more and man of the match, Derek Johnstone had the teams level when he crashed home an unstoppable shot. Now there could only be one winner. Rangers had Celtic on the run. Cooper began to sparkle on the wing and only two excellent saves from Latchford kept him from scoring. Rangers were well on top but found the Celtic 'keeper in defiant mood. Time was running out, when, with only nine minutes remaining, the big Englishman made his only mistake and there was Gordon Smith to knock in the winner in an 'Old Firm' debut he will never forget.

The 3-2 victory proved to be a turning point in Rangers' season. They went on to win the 'treble', winning the League from Aberdeen by two points, beating the 'Dons' 2-1 in the Scottish Cup Final and Celtic 2-1 in the League Cup Final, with Smith again scoring the winner.

Rangers: McCloy; Jardine, Forsyth, Johnstone, Miller; Russell, MacDonald (McLean), McKean, Parlane (Greig), Smith, Cooper.

Celtic: Latchford; McGrain, MacDonald, Casey, Lynch; Edvaldsson, Dowie (McAdam), Burns (Lennox); Doyle, Glavin, Wilson.

RANGERS FUN QUIZ

Test your knowledge of Rangers stars and scores past and present in this set of 20 teasing questions. You'll find the answers on page 62 – but no cheating by looking first!

Goalscorers

1. Who was Rangers' leading goalscorer in season 1990/91?

2. Name the Ranger who scored hat-tricks in his first two games for Rangers in 1967/68.

3. Who was top goalscorer in the successful 1971/72 European Cup Winners' Cup campaign?

4. Who scored Rangers' goal at Pittodrie in the 1986/87 League Championship decider?

5. David Dodds scored one first-team goal in 1990/91 — against whom?

Grounds

6. Name the stadium where Rangers won the European Cup Winners' Cup in 1972.

7. At which ground did Rangers clinch the 1989/90 League Championship?

8. Name the London ground where Rangers played two European ties.

9. Rangers played a European Cup tie at a stadium named after which American president?

10. May 15th Stadium — who did Rangers play in a European tie at this venue?

Captains

11. Who was the last Rangers captain to lift the Scottish Cup?

12. Rangers won the League Cup six times during the 1980s, with five different captains — can you name them?

13. Which Rangers skipper was nicknamed 'Corky'?

14. Who captained Rangers in the 1967 European Cup Winners' Cup final in Nuremberg?

15. Who did John Greig first appoint as his club captain on becoming manager?

Cup Finals

16. Who scored a historic penalty for Rangers in the 1928 Scottish Cup Final?

17. Four goals in a League Cup Final — which Rangers player achieved that notable feat?

18. Rangers' first European final was in 1960/61 — who scored Rangers' goal in the 1-4 aggregate defeat by Fiorentina?

19. Name the contestants when the Scottish Cup Final was last held at Ibrox Stadium.

20. Three former Rangers players won Scottish Cup medals with Motherwell in 1991 — can you identify them?

TOM FORSYTH

THERE have been very few more popular Rangers players during the last two decades than Tom Forsyth — a fearsome competitor. Strong, hard, but fair in the tackle with good distribution, he truly played for the jersey.

Born on 23rd January 1949, Forsyth's career started at Stonehouse Violet, before joining Motherwell in 1967, where he made his name primarily as a midfield player. While at Motherwell Tom won one cap for Scotland against Denmark in 1971 (a 1-0 defeat in Copenhagen), as well as playing for the Scottish League side which lost by the same score later that year to England at Hampden.

Five years later the result was repeated when Forsyth played in the very last such fixture. His later years at Fir Park saw him drifting back to play in central defence and it was for this position that he was signed for Rangers by Jock Wallace in October 1972 for a £45,000 fee. He made his debut four days later in a 2-0 win at Motherwell of all places!

His arrival at Ibrox coincided with a Rangers revival. A long unbeaten run followed, encompassing 26 games, which saw Rangers just fail to wrest the league title from Celtic by one point. However, success came in the Centenary Scottish Cup Final in the presence of Her Royal Highness The Princess Alexandra, with a 3-2 win over Celtic in as dramatic a final as Hampden had witnessed for many a long day.

The score was level at 2-2, with the clock just past the hour mark when Tom Forsyth scored his first-ever goal for Rangers — one of the most famous in Scottish Cup history — from all of six inches, with probably the studs on the sole of his boot, after a Derek Johnstone header from a Tommy McLean free kick had hit both posts. It just had to be the winner, and it was. . . .

That first Scottish Cup medal was followed by three others (1975, 1976 and 1981), three League Championship medals and two for the League Cup, in an Ibrox career spanning 324 competitive games.

Twenty-one Scotland caps were bestowed on Forsyth whilst a Ranger, the most memorable of which was the Scotland-England meeting at Hampden in 1976. Disparaging remarks had been made by Tommy Docherty, likening the comparison between Tom Forsyth and Martin Buchan to that of a carthorse and a thoroughbred!

Undaunted, Forsyth played superbly well at the heart of the Scottish defence, saving the day in the dying seconds when, with Mike Channon clean through on goal, he produced a quite magnificent tackle to win the ball.

Perhaps his finest display in a Rangers jersey was on the occasion of the 1975/76 League Cup Final when Forsyth completely nullified the threat from Kenny Dalglish. His performance, together with that of Captain John Greig, inspired Rangers to a 1-0 win over Celtic.

Injury problems beset his later career, his absence almost certainly costing Rangers the League Championship of 1978/79, and he was finally forced to admit defeat in March 1982, retiring from the game. His loss to Rangers was perhaps unquantifiable. The club rightly awarded him a testimonial match against Swansea City one year later.

A three-year spell as manager of Dunfermline Athletic followed, before he teamed up again with Tommy McLean at Motherwell, as assistant manager, the partnership bearing fruit in the Scottish Cup success of 1991.

Tom Forsyth makes his crucial tackle on Mike Channon in the Scotland-England game at Hampden in 1976 to stop an almost certain goal. Alan Rough is the keeper and a clean-shaven Danny McGrain is in the background.

INTERNATIONAL FOOTBALL RETURNS TO IBROX

A gap of more than fifty years was closed on February 6th 1991, on the historic occasion of the Soviet Union's visit to Glasgow to face Scotland in the first full Category 'A' International to be played at Ibrox Stadium since World War II.

March 1889 had been the date of the very first Rangers-hosted international, with Scotland defeating Ireland 7-0 at Old Ibrox Park before 5,000 spectators, the first of six visits to the Rangers ground by the Irish, each one resulting in a Scottish victory.

Wales came on three occasions and England twice. Their appearance in 1892 resulted in a decisive 4-1 triumph for the 'Auld Enemy', who led 4-0 at half-time, watched by an attendance of 21,000.

England's second visit, on April 5th 1902, was the first international to be staged at the site of the present Ibrox Stadium, but tragically will only be remembered for it being the occasion of the First Ibrox Disaster, 26 people falling to their deaths when the wooden terracing at the West End of the ground collapsed.

75,000 had been inside Ibrox that day. As a result of the disaster Rangers' ground, along with almost every other, would have to be reconstructed on safer lines.

One of the most remarkable of the series was the Victory International of March 1919, when Scotland defeated Ireland 2-1 before 50,000 spectators, thanks to two goals from Andy Wilson of Hearts, who had sustained a wartime injury of a shattered left arm in 1918.

Incredibly, Scotland started this match with just NINE men. Alex McNair and Jimmy McMullan had been stranded by a railway breakdown, although both did appear after ten minutes play.

Although Ireland and Wales were regular visitors at Ibrox until 1931, the shrinking globe was bringing contact with the footballing nations of Europe more into focus, and thus Germany faced Scotland at Ibrox Stadium in October 1936.

Canada had gone down 1-5 at Old Ibrox in 1891, but the pride of the Fatherland were the first European nation to play on the hallowed turf.

It was a remarkable day all things considered, with the Nazi swastika flying over Ibrox. Demonstrators outside the ground urged a boycott of the fixture, but 61,000 witnessed a fine 2-0 home win, with Jimmy Delaney scoring both goals.

The last Category 'A' International until recently took place in December 1938, when Scotland defeated the Magyars of Hungary 3-1 on a bleak winter's day which marked the solitary international appearance of Scot Symon, who achieved the notable feat of representing Scotland at both football and cricket — since equalled by Andy Goram.

Although not a full Category 'A' fixture, one final international was played at Ibrox in March 1956, when Scotland entertained South Africa before 45,000 spectators to raise funds for the British Olympic Association.

There was keen interest in this game with Rangers stars Don Kitchenbrand and Johnny Hubbard in the Springbok side — indeed, Hubbard scored with a penalty, although Scotland won 2-1.

And so to February 1991, and the return of international football to Ibrox Stadium.

An impressive 20,763 spectators sampled the delights of the facilities at Britain's finest arena on a bitterly cold evening, with Richard Gough honoured to be captain of Scotland — the first Rangers player to lead his country since Graeme Souness in 1986, and the sixth to do so in an international at Ibrox.

The visitors threatened three times in five minutes early on, when first Shalimov shot wastefully wide, then Steve Nicol blocked a close range drive by Kanchelskis, and Andy Goram foiled Yuran.

Gordon Strachan, on duty for the first time in 18 months, was among the best of the Scots, but it was Paul McStay who released Ally McCoist to force Uvarov's only first-half save.

After the interval, Gary McAllister had a shot unluckily deflected by a Soviet head, before substitute Dimitri Kuznetsov side-footed home a last-minute winner.

SCOTLAND: Goram (Hibernian), Malpas (Dundee United), Nicol (Liverpool), McCall (Everton) [McAllister (Leeds United)], Gough (Rangers), McLeish (Aberdeen) [McPherson (Hearts)], Strachan (Leeds United), Fleck (Norwich City) [Durie (Chelsea)], McCoist (Rangers), McStay (Celtic), Boyd (Motherwell) [MacLeod (Hibernian)].

Another Skol Cup Triumph!

The League Cup (as traditionalists prefer to call it) had been a good tournament for Rangers under Graeme Souness — three wins in four seasons, and, even earlier, six triumphs in all during the 1980s.

Indeed, the Souness years had seen the Light Blues contest each and every final, with the last three all being against Aberdeen, who had secured victory in a dramatic extra-time finale by 2-1 in season 1989/90.

This time, however, the enemy was a different, but familiar, one — Celtic — Rangers' greatest

rivals, and a club hungry for success after a barren season.

The omens were not good for the Ibrox men, moreover: captain Terry Butcher was absent, principally due to a rift with his manager — a rift which was eventually to send him to Coventry. New signing Oleg Kuznetsov had suffered a knee injury in only his second game in light blue that would keep him on the sidelines for the entire season; and Maurice Johnston was an eleventh-hour casualty, having taken a bad knock in Belgrade just four days earlier, where Rangers had suffered a 3-0 trouncing at the hands of Red Star.

A goalless first-half was a fair reflection of the play, although Rangers had a seemingly certain penalty claim denied in 27 minutes when Ally McCoist was felled by Pat Bonner. Referee Jim McCluskey waved play on — to the anguish of the light blue legions in the 62,817 Hampden audience.

Mark Hateley was in outstanding form that day, in what was his fourth appearance at the old arena, his titanic struggle with Paul Elliott being at the very heart of the battle. Indeed, Elliott denied his countryman perhaps the best chance of the first-half with a superbly timed tackle and then scored himself in 52 minutes to give Celtic the lead.

The goal arrived following a corner, when a John Collins shot seemed to be covered by Chris Woods, only for Elliott to stoop low and net with an opportunist header.

Celtic seemed in control, but an inexplicable substitution by Billy McNeill tossed away that advantage when he brought on Chris Morris for Joe Miller.

Within five minutes Rangers had replaced Terry Hurlock with Pieter Huistra and the pendulum was swinging towards Ibrox.

With 25 minutes left on the clock, it was all square once more when Mark Hateley outjumped Paul Elliott and headed the ball

down to Ally McCoist, who in turn laid it off for Mark Walters to net with a low drive from 20 yards.

Rangers drove on for the winner, but the final went into extra-time for the second successive year.

Jacki Dziekanowski missed a glorious opportunity for Celtic in the early stages of extra-time, but it was Rangers captain, Richard Gough, who had the final say.

A long free-kick from Gary Stevens found Hateley yet again distracting Elliott and as the Celtic defence hesitated, the Ibrox skipper pounced to steer the ball into the net.

It was a proud moment for Gough when he held aloft the League and Skol Cups — he had known "final failure" before with Dundee United and Tottenham Hotspur as well as Rangers. The occasion was hopefully a foretaste of success in years to come, with Richard now officially Club Captain in succession to Terry Butcher.

TEAMS

RANGERS: Woods, Stevens, Munro, Gough, Spackman, Brown, Steven, Hurlock (Huistra), McCoist (Ferguson), Hateley, Walters.

CELTIC: Bonner, Grant, Wdowczyk, Fulton (Hewitt), Elliott, Rogan, Miller (Morris), McStay, Dziekanowski, Creaney, Collins.

Skol Cup Final action: Mark Walters equalises . . . and Packie Bonner literally goes overboard after clashing with Ally McCoist.

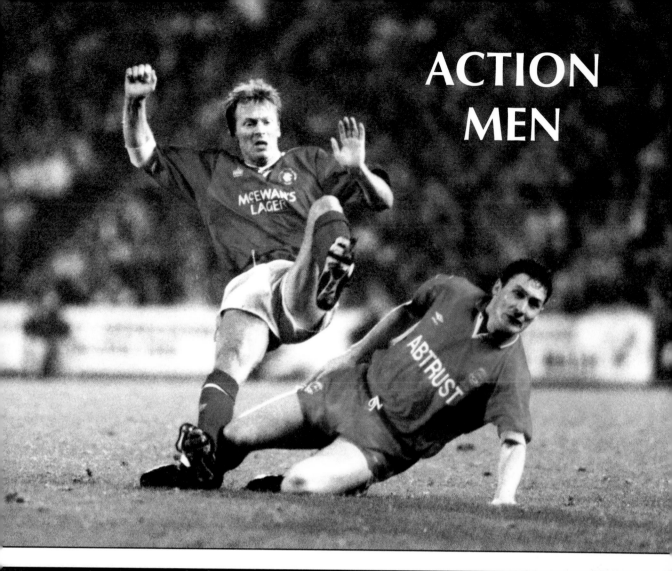

ACTION MEN

WILLIE THORNTON

A typical Willie Thornton goal, as another great header powers into the net. This one marked a hat-trick in the Cup semi-final against East Fife in March 1949.

THERE have been many fine headers of a ball who have worn Rangers colours — in the post-war era such as Jimmy Millar, Derek Johnstone and most recently Mark Hateley all spring to mind; but there would be few quibbles if you were to rate Willie Thornton as the finest of them all.

Born in Winchburgh, West Lothian, on March 3rd 1920, Willie played for the local Albion before signing amateur forms with Rangers in March 1936. He made his first team debut on January 2nd 1937 (before his 17th birthday!) at Firhill, playing at outside-right in a 1-0 Rangers win, thus becoming one of the youngest-ever to play for the Light Blues. He turned professional on his birthday.

Five league games were played in that inaugural season of 1936/37 and Willie was a regular by the following term, scoring eight goals in twenty

appearances, his first coming in a home league game versus St Johnstone on August 28th 1937 in a 2-2 draw.

Even then, in the pre-war era, the teenage Thornton was teaming up with another youngster with whom he would be inextricably linked for so long — a certain Willie Waddell. In the late '40s and early '50s that partnership would combine to devastating effect for Rangers, Waddell's thundering runs on the right wing time after time ending in the cross being converted by Thornton's head.

Not that Thornton's only asset was his head — predominantly a right-sided player, he was skilful, a good passer of the ball, with a keen football brain and an expert at snapping up even a half chance.

Like so many of his contemporaries, his career was interrupted by the outbreak of war in 1939 and Willie Thornton was to serve with distinction in the colours of the Duke of Atholl's Scottish Horse Regiment in places like Cairo, Tripoli, Anzio and Monte Cassino, winning the Military Medal for his actions in Sicily on November 18th 1943.

Football was not entirely forgotten during the war. Playing first of all as a guest with Norwich City for five games, he later appeared alongside such as Tom Finney and George Hamilton for the Army's Central Mediterranean team.

The Victory Internationals of 1946 brought Willie his first international appearance, playing for Scotland against Switzerland on May 15th in a 3-1 win at Hampden. His second international call came in August of that same year, when he scored both goals in Scotland's 2-2 draw with England at Maine Road, Manchester, in a game specially arranged to raise money for the Bolton Disaster Fund.

Seven full international appearances followed, which many observers felt was too few by far for a player of Willie's class. His tally of medals at club level in the blue of Rangers makes impressive reading — four League Championships (including one pre-war), three Scottish Cups and three League Cups. A member of the Rangers team which won the inaugural League Cup in 1946/47 and which achieved, two years on, Scotland's very first 'treble' success, Thornton scored a career total of 254 goals in 431 games for Rangers.

Not once during a first-team playing career that spanned the years 1937-1954 was Willie Thornton ordered off or even booked — a record of which he is justifiably proud and which earned him the title 'Player of the Year' in 1952.

Retiring in June 1954, Willie retained his links with football through management and journalism. As manager of Dundee from 1954-1959 he introduced such young talent as Andy Penman, Alan Gilzean, Alan Cousins, Jim Gabriel, Alex Hamilton and Ian Ure to the Dens Park club, laying the foundation for that club's League Championship success in 1961/62.

The death in office of his old mentor David Meiklejohn at Partick Thistle led to Thornton's move to Firhill as manager in September 1959, a post he was to hold for nine years before returning to Ibrox as assistant, firstly to David White, then to Willie Waddell.

One unique distinction from that period is his 100% record as Rangers manager. Being acting manager for two games between White's departure and Waddell's arrival, Willie led the team in two winning matches, giving him a record unlikely ever to be equalled!

Willie Thornton died on 26th August 1991.

To the end he remained at Ibrox as custodian of the Trophy Room and host of the Thornton Suite on matchdays. He had nothing but happy memories of more than half a century in football, right back to the time when the formidable Bill Struth doubled the teenage Thornton's wage packet on the strength of his boots being so clean!

A unique photo of Willie in the dug-out during his two-match spell as acting manager. Who's the Joe Miller look-alike at top right, we wonder?

Rangers v Nice

October/November 1956

Rangers defenders Young, Logie and Caldow and goalkeeper George Niven guard against a Nice cross.

Our First Foray into Europe!

THE European Cup was one year old — already it had captured the imagination of clubs and spectators alike all over the Continent and season 1956/57 saw Rangers make their debut.

A first-round bye meant the Ibrox men were paired with O.G.C. Nice in the second round, with the first leg scheduled for Ibrox on October 24th 1956.

An attendance of 65,000 produced an electrifying atmosphere with the contrast in styles making for an engrossing contest. Rangers were the more powerful direct side playing very much in typical British fashion. The French champions played in the Latin style and the different interpretation of the laws of the game would lead, over the course of the tie, to many flashpoints and heated incidents.

Nice drew first blood in 23 minutes, when Faivre opened the scoring. Only a superb display of goalkeeping by Colonna, aided by resolute defending from his colleagues and some bad finishing from the Rangers forwards, kept the score the same until close to half-time, when a Max Murray header levelled matters.

Rangers laid siege to the French goal in the second-half but had only a Billy Simpson goal on the hour mark to show for it, in a period remarkable for two incidents directly related to referee Arthur Ellis of Halifax. In 55 minutes he called both sets of players together to deliver a lecture (he later admitted that his main concern was the body-checking by the French) and then, with five minutes of playing time still left, he blew for full-time. Upon realising his error, Mr Ellis recalled both teams — in Eric Caldow's case from the bath — to finish the game!

The return game in Nice was set for November 1st, but torrential rain forced its cancellation — this on the Cote d'Azure! Yet more rain greeted Rangers when they returned to the French Riviera on November 14th, but this time the game went ahead on a quagmire of a pitch, with the heavy conditions suiting the Scots.

Only crude tackling stopped Rangers time and time again as they dominated play, until the 40th minute, when Gonzales fouled Murray once too often and a brave referee awarded a penalty. Despite protestation from the entire French team, South African Johnny Hubbard made his customarily efficient job from the spot.

Rangers remained on top for much of the second half, with Sammy Baird and Max Murray most prominent, but chances aplenty were scorned and a mishit shot by Bravo on the hour was followed within two minutes by a Foix conversion from a cross by Faivre and suddenly the aggregate score was level. The tie was to finish with both sides reduced to ten men following a flare-up between Logie and Bravo in the closing minutes. A third match was to be held in Paris.

The Colombes Stadium was the venue two weeks later, attracting a 15,000 attendance in the French capital. Yet again Rangers dominated the first half without having anything to show for it, with Colonna again producing some superb saves. Almost on the half-time whistle, a Nice breakaway saw Ujlak releasing Foix, who netted from 12 yards.

Rangers struck back soon after the interval when a hard, low cross from Sammy Baird was turned into his own net by Bonvin, only for Muro to restore the French lead within minutes, taking advantage of a defensive blunder to net.

The die was cast and Faivre added a third before the end to put Rangers out of the European Cup.

Thus ended Rangers' very first European sojourn — there would be many, many more to follow, but none quite like that three-match . tussle which encompassed three cities, three trips to France by Rangers, ten goals and four orderings-off.

The Race to Sweden

Rangers Stars involved in European Championship Action

Rangers had been well-represented at the 1990 World Cup in Italy in both the Scottish and English squads, with a record seven players taking part; and the onset of the European Championship at the start of season 1990/91 was eagerly awaited in the Ibrox dressing-room.

Captain Terry Butcher, who led England to the World Cup semi-finals, had intimated his retirement from international football, as had Maurice Johnston for Scotland following the Italian campaign. Johnston was later to reverse this controversial decision, only for illness and injury to deprive him of the opportunity to add to his fourteen goals for Scotland, at least until 1991/92.

Richard Gough, captain of Rangers and Scotland.

Scotland's opening European Championship fixture was scheduled for Hampden Park on the night of September 12th 1990, with Romania the attractive opposition.

A miserable 12,801 attendance was attracted to the old ground, reflecting the effects of live television and the lack of confidence in the Scottish team, who had never before qualified for the European Championship finals.

Such pessimism was, however, misplaced, as Scotland came from behind to record a fine 2-1 victory. Lone Ranger Ally McCoist played a prominent part, flicking on a Gary McAllister cross for John Robertson to net in 37 minutes and then scoring the winner himself just a quarter of an hour from the end from a Robertson cross laid off by Tom Boyd.

Switzerland were the next visitors to Mount Florida just five weeks later, with Ally McCoist again in dark blue colours.

Encouraged by the fine opening win, 27,740 spectators were in attendance, only for the Ranger to miss a penalty, firing wide after himself being fouled.

Scotland nevertheless went on to record another 2-1 win, John Robertson and Gary McAllister being the goalscorers.

That same evening, Chris Woods kept goal for England at Wembley in a 2-0 victory over Poland before a massive 77,040 crowd. Gary Lineker and Peter Beardsley were the goalscorers, in their country's opening European Championship fixture.

Woods retained his place for England's next match against the Republic of Ireland in Dublin on November 14th, as the two protagonists renewed hostilities following their World Cup clash. Woods again had an outstanding game, as England gained a valuable point in a 1-1 draw, David Platt netting.

That same afternoon, Scotland took a major step towards Sweden by snatching a point in a 1-1 draw with Bulgaria in Sofia, before 42,000 fans. Ally McCoist opened the scoring in nine minutes, when Gordon Durie knocked back a Tommy Boyd cross for him to net.

Intense second-half pressure saw the Bulgarians finally equalise in 70 minutes, but Scotland held on for a vital point.

The return leg was held at Hampden on March 27th 1991. On this occasion Ally McCoist was joined by his club captain Richard Gough, making his only European Championship appearance of the season, being plagued for much of the term by illness and injury (although he did captain Scotland in the Ibrox international versus the USSR).

The result was again a 1-1 draw, Emil Kostadinov snatching a last-minute equaliser after John Collins had put Scotland ahead just five minutes earlier, watched by a crowd of 33,119.

At Wembley that same evening the scoreline was also 1-1, with England and Eire still unable to produce a winner.

Lee Dixon was the goalscorer for England before another 77,000 attendance, but on this occasion the new England manager, Graham Taylor, inexplicably left Chris Woods out of the team, despite the fact that the Ranger had never let his country down.

Ally McCoist has been a regular scorer for Scotland in recent years.

Pieter Huistra joined his Ibrox colleagues in the European Championship arena on April 17th 1991, playing for Holland in a 2-0 win over Finland in Rotterdam before 27,000 spectators. Marco van Basten and Ruud Gullit scored the goals that placed Holland at the head of their section, one point clear of Portugal.

The final European Championship fixtures of season 1990/91 took place on May 1st. Scotland won 2-0 in San Marino, thanks to goals by Gordon Strachan and Gordon Durie, and England dumped Turkey 1-0 in Istanbul thanks to a Dennis Wise counter. Both matches were devoid of any Ibrox influence.

England's win left them leaders of their group, one point clear of the Republic of Ireland and Poland thanks to those countries' goalless draw in Dublin that same afternoon. With Scotland also in pole position in their section, the hope for all Rangers fans must be that Scotland, England and the Netherlands will all qualify for "Sweden 1992", with each squad suitably embellished with Rangers players!

RANGERS PRIZE QUIZ

Test your knowledge of 'Old Firm' facts and win an autographed copy of "BLUE HEAVEN, The Ibrox Trophy Room" by Rangers legend, Willie Thornton. The new 112-page book (see Page 64), recently published by Holmes McDougall, is a fascinating record of the major trophies and gifts housed at Ibrox Stadium. The first TEN all-correct entries drawn from the assembled competition mail will all receive a special copy of this unique publication.

The
'Old Firm'

1. Encompassing all games, name the player who is the all-time leading goalscorer for Rangers in 'Old Firm' meetings.

2. At which venue did Rangers defeat Celtic 3-1 to win the 1901 Glasgow Exhibition Cup Final?

3. Name the Rangers player who made his debut against Celtic in a Scottish Cup Final.

4. In which tournament did Rangers secure their first-ever victory over Celtic?

5. Only one Rangers player has scored more than one hat-trick in an 'Old Firm' game — can you name him?

6. The record attendance for Ibrox Stadium is 118,567 — against Celtic — in which year?

7. Before Maurice Johnston, who was the last player to play for both Rangers and Celtic?

8. What is Rangers' record score in all games against Celtic?

9. Name the only pair of brothers to play for Rangers against Celtic.

10. Encompassing all games, name the Ranger who has made most appearances of all-time in 'Old Firm' meetings.

RULES and CONDITIONS: The closing date for entries is 29th February 1992. NO ENTRIES RECEIVED AFTER THAT DATE WILL BE ACCEPTED. The Winners will be the first 10 all-correct entries drawn from the assembled mail and the lucky entrants will be notified as soon as possible after the closing date.

Entries should be addressed to "RANGERS OLD FIRM QUIZ", Holmes McDougall Limited, 137-141 Leith Walk, Edinburgh EH6 8NS and must clearly show the Entrant's Name and Address.

The Editors' decision is final and strictly no correspondence will be entered into.

This competition is not open to employees (or the families of employees) of either Holmes McDougall Limited or Rangers Football Club.

Fun Quiz answers — how many did you get right?

Goalscorers
1. Maurice Johnston (19)
2. Colin Stein
3. Colin Stein (5)
4. Terry Butcher
5. Valetta

Grounds
6. Nou Camp Stadium, Barcelona
7. Tannadice Park, Dundee
8. Arsenal Stadium, Highbury
9. Franklyn D. Roosevelt
10. Ankaragucu (Turkey)

Captains
11. Ally Dawson (1981)
12. Sandy Jardine, John McClelland, Craig Paterson, Terry Butcher, Graham Roberts
13. George Young
14. John Greig
15. Derek Johnstone

Cup Finals
16. David Meiklejohn
17. Jim Forrest (v Morton 1963/64)
18. Alex Scott
19. Airdrieonians 2 Hibernian 0 (1924)
20. Craig Paterson, Davie Cooper, Ian Ferguson

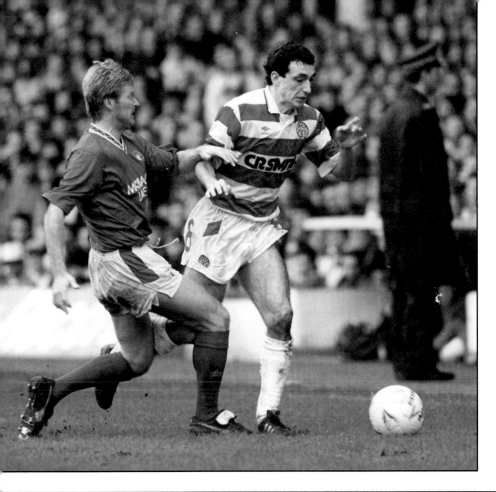

OLD
FIRM
ACTION

BLUE HEAVEN
The Ibrox Trophy Room
by Willie Thornton

A unique guide to the fabulous collection of trophies & gifts housed at Ibrox Stadium, written by a true Rangers legend (see Page 56) and with a Foreword by Chairman, David Murray.

AVAILABLE NOW! from Rangers Shops, John Menzies, good bookshops or direct from the Publishers, Holmes McDougall. Send your cheque, credit card details or P.O. for £13.95 (Paperback) or £19.95 (Hardback) to:

"BLUE HEAVEN",

Holmes McDougall Ltd,

Publishing Division,

137-141 Leith Walk,

EDINBURGH,

EH6 8NS.

or

Telephone:

(031) 554 9444

for Immediate

Despatch by

ordering on Mastercard/Visa/Access.

ACKNOWLEDGEMENTS

Published by Holmes McDougall Limited, Allander House, 137-141 Leith Walk, Edinburgh EH6 8NS, Scotland.

Printed and bound in Scotland.
Edited by Douglas Russell and John Traynor (Holmes McDougall Limited).
Written by Robert McElroy of "The Rangers Historian".
Page layout by Roger Smith.
Origination by Centre Graphics, Livingston.
Typesetting by Trinity Typesetting, Edinburgh.

All photographs supplied by *The Evening Times*.

Every effort has been made by the publishers to ensure the accuracy of all details and information in this publication.